Magento 1.3 Sales Tactics Cookbook

Improve your Magento store's sales and increase your profits with this collection of simple and effective tactical techniques

William Rice

BIRMINGHAM - MUMBAI

Magento 1.3 Sales Tactics Cookbook

First published: April 2010

Production Reference: 1220310

Published by Packt Publishing Ltd.
32 Lincoln Road
Olton
Birmingham, B27 6PA, UK.

ISBN 978-1-849510-12-7

www.packtpub.com

Cover Image by Ed Maclean (edmaclean@gmail.com)

Credits

Author
William Rice

Reviewer
Jose Argudo Blanco

Acquisition Editor
David Barnes

Development Editor
Mehul Shetty

Technical Editor
Alfred John

Copy Editor
Leonard D'silva

Indexer
Hemangini Bari

Editorial Team Leader
Aanchal Kumar

Project Team Leader
Priya Mukherji

Project Coordinator
Ashwin Shetty

Proofreaders
Lynda Sliwoski

Lesley Harrison

Production Coordinators
Adline Swetha Jesuthas

Melwyn D'sa

Cover Work
Adline Swetha Jesuthas

About the Author

William Rice is a software training professional who lives, works, and plays in New York City. He is the author of books on Moodle, Magento, and software training.

His indoor hobbies include writing books and spending way too much time reading sites like Slashdot (www.slashdot.org). His outdoor hobbies include orienteering, foraging for wild edibles in New York City parks, and practicing archery within site of JFK Airport.

William is fascinated by the relationship between technology and society: how we create our tools, and how our tools in turn shape us. He is married to an incredible woman who encourages his writing pursuits and has two amazing sons.

William can be contacted through his blog at http://williamriceinc.blogspot.com.

A huge "thank you" to my wife, for giving me the time and space to complete this book. And to my in-laws for their support during this project. An overdue thank you to David Barnes for recruiting me into the Packt family.

About the Reviewer

Jose Argudo is a web developer from Valencia, Spain. After finishing his studies, he started working for a web design company. After six years of working for that company, and others, he decided to start working as a freelancer.

Now, he thinks it's the best decision he has ever made, a decision that lets him work with the tools he likes, such as Joomla!, CodeIgniter, CakePHP, jQuery, and other known open source technologies.

His desire to learn and share his knowledge has led him to be a regular reviewer of books from Packt, such as *Drupal E-commerce, Joomla With Flash, Joomla! 1.5 SEO, Magento 1.3 Theme Design,* and *Symfony 1.3 Web Application Development.*

Recently he has even published his own book, *Codeigniter 1.7,* which you can also find at Packt Publishing's site. If you work with PHP...take a look at it.

If you want to know more about him, you can check his website www.joseargudo.com.

To my brother, I wish him the best.

For my son Liam, whose enthusiasm for life and sense of wonder renewed my own.

Table of Contents

Preface

Magento is a feature-rich, professional open source e-commerce solution that offers users complete flexibility and control over the look, content, and functionality of their online store. Although Magento provides users with the power to create dynamic e-commerce sites, it can be challenging to get beyond the basics and create sites that are tailored to your unique business needs.

This book gives you a hands-on experience with Magento, helping you increase your revenue by implementing proven sales tactics on your Magento site.

After creating an online store with Magento, you will follow a defined series of steps to boost revenues on your site. By following straightforward instructions, you can implement proven e-commerce sales techniques. You will learn to customize the default Magento storefront so that it becomes your store and also learn about Magento's directory structure and where some of the elements of a store are customized. As you work your way through each chapter, your store will grow in scope and sophistication. By the time you finish this book, your online store will be optimized for maximum sales.

What this book covers

Chapter 1, Attracting Visitors shows you how to increase the traffic to your store by adding meta information, optimizing images for search engines, using title prefix or suffix to add the store name to page titles, generating a site map, and configuring Magento to automatically refresh the site map.

Chapter 2, Placing Products on Shopping Sites shows you how to place products on shopping sites.

Chapter 3, Driving Visitors to Your Product Pages shows you how to customize Magento's default CMS pages, create new CMS pages, decide which About pages to include, and decide what content to include on About pages.

Chapter 4, Making the Sale by Optimizing Product Pages walks you through the various techniques to optimize product pages such as adding custom options, adding video, links, and other HTML to product pages, optimizing product images, telling a story using product images, and changing the layout of a product page.

Chapter 5, Increasing the Sale guides you through the various techniques for maximizing sales by upselling, making additional sales with related products and custom options, and offering cross-sells, quantity discounts and free shipping.

Chapter 6, Offering and Advertising Promotions shows you how to offer promotional pricing by using catalog price rule and shopping cart price rule.

Chapter 7, Engage Your Customers shows you how to engage your customers by customizing transactional e-mails, creating and sending newsletter, and choosing the social networking site.

Chapter 8, Let Your Customers Speak guides you through the various tools such as reviews, ratings, polls, tags, and e-mail to a friend that enable your customers to communicate with you and others.

Chapter 9, Internationalization shows you how to prepare your site for international sales by translating your products and CMS pages, creating a new URL for your international store, and customizing transactional emails for your international store.

Chapter 10, Create a Wholesale Store shows you how to create a wholesale store for wholesale customers.

What you need for this book

You need Magento, installed either on your local machine or on a remote server, and your favorite code editor.

Who this book is for

If you are a Magento store owner or store designer who wants to boost sales with these tactics, then this book is for you.

Conventions

In this book, you will find a number of styles of text that distinguish between different kinds of information. Here are some examples of these styles, and an explanation of their meaning.

Code words in text are shown as follows: "Open the file `robots.txt` for editing."

A block of code is set as follows:

```
<?php endforeach ?>
</tbody>
</table>
<h3 align='center'>Use the Share Wishlist button below to ask friends
to subscribe to your wishlist. When they subscribe, they will be
notified whenever you update your wishlist.</h3>
<script type='text/javascript'>decorateTable('wishlist-table')</
script>
<div class='button-set'>
```

When we wish to draw your attention to a particular part of a code block, the relevant lines or items are set in bold:

```
<?php endforeach ?>
</tbody>
</table>
<h3 align='center'>Use the Share Wishlist button below to ask friends
to subscribe to your wishlist. When they subscribe, they will be
notified whenever you update your wishlist.</h3>
<script type='text/javascript'>decorateTable('wishlist-table')</
script>
<div class='button-set'>
```

New terms and important words are shown in bold. Words that you see on the screen, in menus or dialog boxes for example, appear in the text like this: "Select the Actions tab".

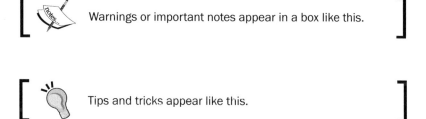

Warnings or important notes appear in a box like this.

Tips and tricks appear like this.

Reader feedback

Feedback from our readers is always welcome. Let us know what you think about this book—what you liked or may have disliked. Reader feedback is important for us to develop titles that you really get the most out of.

To send us general feedback, simply send an e-mail to feedback@packtpub.com, and mention the book title via the subject of your message.

If there is a book that you need and would like to see us publish, please send us a note in the **SUGGEST A TITLE** form on www.packtpub.com or e-mail suggest@packtpub.com.

If there is a topic that you have expertise in and you are interested in either writing or contributing to a book on, see our author guide on www.packtpub.com/authors.

Customer support

Now that you are the proud owner of a Packt book, we have a number of things to help you to get the most from your purchase.

Errata

Although we have taken every care to ensure the accuracy of our content, mistakes do happen. If you find a mistake in one of our books—maybe a mistake in the text or the code—we would be grateful if you would report this to us. By doing so, you can save other readers from frustration and help us improve subsequent versions of this book. If you find any errata, please report them by visiting http://www.packtpub.com/support, selecting your book, clicking on the let us know link, and entering the details of your errata. Once your errata are verified, your submission will be accepted and the errata will be uploaded on our website, or added to any list of existing errata, under the Errata section of that title. Any existing errata can be viewed by selecting your title from http://www.packtpub.com/support.

Piracy

Piracy of copyrighted material on the Internet is an ongoing problem across all media. At Packt, we take the protection of our copyright and licenses very seriously. If you come across any illegal copies of our works, in any form, on the Internet, please provide us with the location address or website name immediately so that we can pursue a remedy.

Please contact us at copyright@packtpub.com with a link to the suspected pirated material.

We appreciate your help in protecting our authors, and our ability to bring you valuable content.

Questions

You can contact us at questions@packtpub.com if you are having a problem with any aspect of the book, and we will do our best to address it.

1

Attracting Visitors

In this chapter, you will learn how to increase the traffic to your site using the following techniques:

- ▶ Add meta information
- ▶ Optimize images for search engines
- ▶ Use title prefix or suffix to add the store name to page titles
- ▶ Generate a site map
- ▶ Configure Magento to automatically refresh the site map

Introduction

Search Engine Optimization (**SEO**) is a technique used to improve a site's performance in search engines. A search engine is a search site like www.google.com, www.bing.com, and www.yahoo.com. According to conventional wisdom, sites that appear near the top of the search results will receive the most clicks.

For example, our demonstration site sells coffee. So we want our site to appear in search results when people search using phrases like "online coffee store" and "mail order coffee". If our site appears in the first ten results for those search phrases, then it will usually be displayed on the first page of results. We would not expect to receive more visitors if our site appeared on the second or later pages.

So let's refine our goal for search engine optimization:

For the search phrases that our potential customers are likely to use, we want our site to appear as high as possible in the search engine results, preferably in the top ten.

There are many books and companies that offer SEO services. Some of them claim to know how the search engines calculate a site's position in the search results, or how to find the most effective search terms for your site. We will keep our claims more modest as compared to that. Instead, this chapter will show you what you can do with Magento to help search engines index your site accurately and completely.

Adding meta information

In this section, we will cover how to optimize your product pages by entering meta information.

The word **meta** means "About this subject". Webmasters use meta tags to tell search engines about a page. A page's meta information should accurately describe the content and purpose of that page. This helps the search engines categorize the page better. Some search engines use meta keywords and meta descriptions, while others ignore them. Because search engines can change their policies at any time, it is to your advantage to add this meta information, just in case your favorite search engine begins using it.

I use the word "page" instead of "site" deliberately. While you may be concerned about the search engine rank of your store's website, search engines do not index sites; they index pages. Therefore, it is important that you try to optimize each page of your store for search engines.

Many store owners are concerned about the search rank of their store's home page. While I do not suggest that you ignore the front page, you should also optimize each product's page. When people search for a specific type of online store, you want your store's front page to rank high in the results. When they search for a specific product, you want at least one of your products to rank high. We will cover optimizing your product pages in another section.

Getting ready

There are three prerequisites for this technique:

- You need access to the administrative interface and must be able to edit product information.
- You must spend time thinking about, and if possible, researching the search terms that your customers will use to find a product.
- You must spend time thinking about, and if possible, researching what your customers want to see in the search results.

How to do it...

1. Log in to your site's backend, or Administrative Panel.

2. Select **Catalog | Manage Products**. The **Manage Products** page displays. A list of the products in your store should appear on this page.

3. Select the product whose meta information you want to edit. The **Product Information** page displays:

4. Select the **Meta Information** tab:

5. In the **Meta Title** field, enter a description title for the product page.

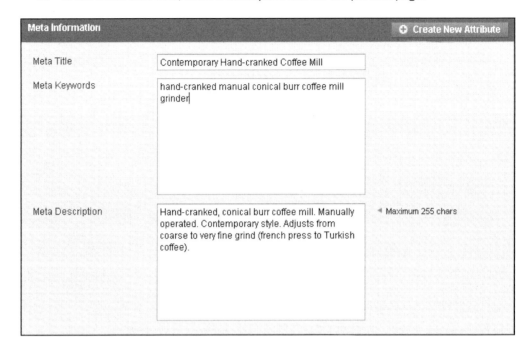

6. In the **Meta Keywords** field, enter the search terms and/or phrases that your customers are most likely to use.

7. In the **Meta Description** field, enter a description that you would like potential customers to see in their search results.

8. Click on the **Save** button.

How it works...

Let's look at how meta information works on a web page.

Meta information and search sites

Here is a product page from our demonstration site:

If you view the HTML code for this page, you will see meta information in several places. You can do this yourself, by selecting **View | Page Source** from your browser's menu.

Near the top of the page, we find the page title which is the first piece of meta information. We also find some meta information that describes the page. We are talking about the title, meta description, and meta keyword tags:

```
<head>
    <title>Blue Mountain Triage--Whole Bean</title>
<meta http-equiv="Content-Type" content="text/html; charset=utf-8" />
<meta name="description" content="The world's most famous coffee, and
for good reason. There are many imitators and blends, but ours is
certified as genuine. Grown only in the Blue Mountains of Jamaica,
between 3,000 and 7,500 feet altitude. Rich, chocolatey,. low in acid
and high in flavor." />
<meta name="keywords" content="Blue Mountain Triage Whole Bean coffee"
/>
```

Search engines use the title and meta tags to categorize a page and to match a person's search terms to your page. No one, except the engineers who create the search engines, knows how much weight is given to each of these elements. However, there is much evidence that meta information plays a part in matching a page to a person's search query. That is why we will carefully construct this meta information for each product page.

> Most SEO experts agree that Google no longer uses the meta keywords tag when ranking search results. However, they do not penalize you for having it, so there's no harm in using it. As of this writing, Yahoo! recommends using it (`http://help.yahoo.com/l/us/yahoo/ search/ranking/ranking-02.html`), and it is still used by some other search engines like AOL.

The title for our example page is **Blue Mountain Triage--Whole Bean**. If someone uses the words in the title in a search, or even better, uses the exact phrase, then the example page should be listed among the results.

In the following screenshot, you can see a very optimistic example. The user has entered the exact search term that we have in our title, and our example page is the first result:

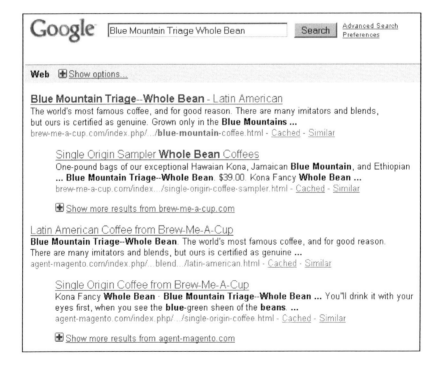

So before you write your title and your meta keywords, spend time thinking about this question:

 What search terms and phrases are most likely to be used by the people who are most likely to buy this product?

The answer is your meta keywords.

Let's take another look at the meta description for this product page:

```
<meta name="description" content="The world's most famous coffee, and
for good reason. There are many imitators and blends, but ours is
certified as genuine. Grown only in the Blue Mountains of Jamaica,
between 3,000 and 7,500 feet altitude. Rich, chocolatey,. low in acid
and high in flavor." />
```

Now, look at the first search result. Sometimes, search engines display the meta description for a page. This means that the person searching will use the meta description to decide whether to visit the page. So before you write your meta description, spend time thinking about this question:

 For the people who are most likely to buy this product, what description will most likely inspire them to visit the product page?

There is much evidence that a page's title has a large effect upon how a search engine categorizes a page, and matches search terms to a page. However, if you stuff a page title with too many keywords, it can become unreadable. So you must also consider this question:

 What page title will accurately describe this product and contain the most productive keywords for customers who search for the product, without becoming too long and unreadable?

Tips for using the most productive keywords, description, and title

In the previous section, we presented several questions that must be answered before adding meta information to your product page. Choosing the best meta information can help customers find your product. How to choose this meta information is the subject of entire books.

Here are some tips for writing meta information:

▸ Don't repeat the same keywords over again because search engines will treat this as spam.

▸ If your title, meta keywords, or meta description tag contains repeated keywords, it might be ignored.

▸ Search engines use a technique called "word stemming". If the person who is searching is looking for a word that is part of one of your keywords, then the search engine will match them. For example, if someone is searching for a "fridge" and one of your keywords is "refrigerator", then the search engine finds that match. So, include the longest form of each search term in your title or meta information.

▸ Try to include the keywords that are in your title and meta information in the body of your page. In Magento, that means repeating the keywords in the Product Description field. We showed you how to do that in the previous section *How to do it....*

If you're interested in learning more about optimizing keywords, descriptions, and titles, then see some of the resources in the following section *There's more....*

There's more...

Because Google has the largest share of the search market, many webmasters are concerned about how their sites rank in Google searches. For advice about optimizing your pages for Google, you can go to Google's help pages.

Webmasters/Site owners help

This is the starting page for webmaster help.

```
http://www.google.com/support/webmasters/
```

Changing a site title and description

This is Google's help page about page titles and descriptions. It gives advice on writing good page titles and descriptions.

```
http://www.google.com/support/webmasters/bin/answer.
py?hl=en&answer=35624
```

Researching keywords

Use the **Keyword** tool to get new keyword ideas.

```
https://adwords.google.com/select/KeywordToolExternal
```

Optimizing images for search engines

Search engines use the information that you enter about images when matching a search query to your page content. In this section, we will see how to optimize image information in Magento so that search engines accurately match searchers with your product page.

We will use the following example page:

Our goal is to optimize the meta information and name of this image, so that it enhances our search value.

How to do it...

Before you log into Magento, rename the image that you want to use on the page. Use a name that describes the product in the picture.

A good name for the image above would be `jamaican-blue-mountain-coffee-whole-bean.jpg`. A bad name for the image above would be `jamaican_flag_with_coffee_beans.jpg`.

1. Log in to your site's backend or Administrative Panel.
2. Select **Catalog | Manage Products**.
3. Select the product whose image information you want to edit.
4. Select the **Image** tab.
5. Select the **Browse Files...** button. A dialog box appears where you will select the image to upload.
6. Navigate to the directory containing the image to upload, and select the image.

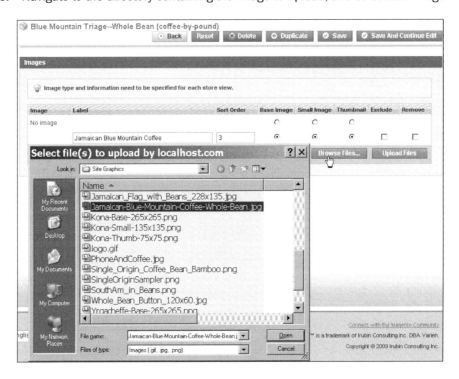

7. With the image selected, click on the **Open** button. The image's filename will be displayed on the page. The image is ready to be uploaded.

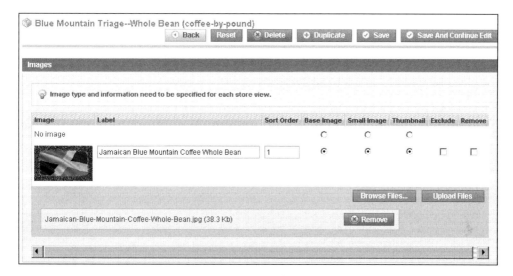

8. Click on the **Upload Files** button, and the image will be added to the page.

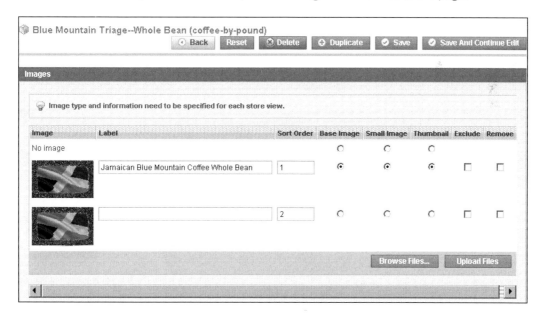

If there is an old image, as in the previous screenshot, you will want to remove it.

Follow these steps:

1. In the row for the old image, enable the **Remove** checkbox.
2. In the row for the new image, click on the radio buttons for the image sizes (**Base Image**, **Small Image**, and **Thumbnail**).
3. In the row for the new image, enter a **Label** for the image. Remember to use keywords that enhance the search result for the page.
4. Click on the **Save** button.

How it works...

Let's take a look at the HTML code for this page. When we view the source code, we see the HTML code that puts the image of the coffee on the page. The image also has meta information, which should describe the picture. Look for the "alt" and "title" text:

```
<img src="http://localhost.com/brew-me-a-cup.com/media/catalog/
product/cache/1/thumbnail/56x/5e06319eda06f020e43594a9c230972d/j/a/
jamaican-blue-mountain-coffee-whole-bean.jpg" alt="Jamaican Blue
Mountain Coffee Whole Bean" title="Jamaican Blue Mountain Coffee Whole
Bean" />
```

Notice that the image's name indicates it is the one we uploaded in the previous instructions. The name contains keywords that accurately describe the content of the picture and the page.

Also notice the alt and title text for the image. Magento used the text we entered into the **Label** field for those tags. Search engines will see those key words, even if your visitors don't.

There's more...

Yahoo! offers tips for improving the search engine ranking of your web pages. You can see the article at `http://help.yahoo.com/l/us/yahoo/search/ranking/ranking-02.html`. Notice the sixth bullet point: "Use ALT text for graphics..."

Google also offers tips for writing good alt text on their page titled *Images* at `http://www.google.com/support/webmasters/bin/answer.py?answer=114016`.

Using title prefix or suffix to add the store name to page titles

In the first section of this chapter *Add meta information*, you saw that search engines use the page title as one of their criteria for ranking a page and matching search queries to that page. You also saw that you enter the page title for a product page. This makes every product page's title unique.

Sometimes, you might want every page in your site to have some common text in its title. For example, you might want every page to have the name of your store. This is especially true when common text is a search term for which you want every page to be shown.

In our demonstration store, we might want "Online Coffee Store" to be added to every page's title. This is a common search phrase that could apply to every page.

You can add a prefix, a suffix, or both to every page's title. The prefix will be added in front of the page title, and the suffix will be added to the end of the page title. In the following screenshot, **Blue Mountain Coffee** is the name of the page. **Online Coffee Store** is a suffix that gets added to the title of every page on the site:

How to do it...

1. Log in to your site's backend, or Administrative Pancl.

2. Select **System | Configuration**. The **Configuration** page displays.

3. From the **General** section, select **Design.** The **Design** page displays.

4. Scroll down to the section for **HTML Head.**

5. Enter the prefix or suffix into the field for **Title Prefix** or **Title Suffix.**

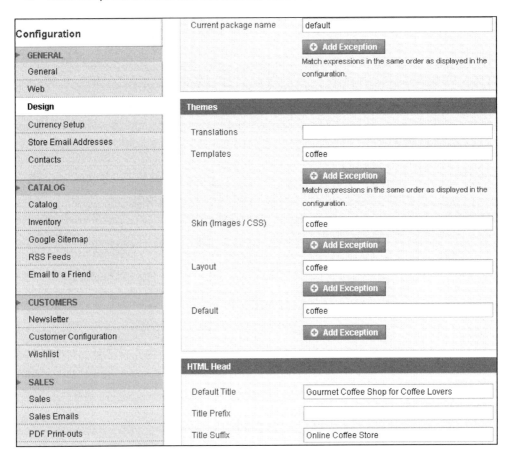

6. Click on the **Save Config** button.

How it works...

Let's take a look at the HTML code for this page. When we view the source code, we see that the suffix has been added to the "title" text:

```
<!DOCTYPE html PUBLIC "-//W3C//DTD XHTML 1.0 Strict//EN" "http://www.
w3.org/TR/xhtml1/DTD/xhtml1-strict.dtd">
<html xmlns="http://www.w3.org/1999/xhtml" xml:lang="en" lang="en">
<head>
    <title> Blue Mountain Coffee Online Coffee Store</title>
```

There's more...

Under **Configuration | General | Design**, scroll further down the page, and you will see a field labeled **Miscellaneous HTML**. This is HTML code that is added to the end of every page in your store.

However, remember that the code doesn't need to be permanent. For example, in our online coffee store, we could put a coffee-related quote in this field, and change the quote whenever we wanted a fresh one. We could add links to websites for coffee lovers. You can add any HTML code here, if you think it will enhance your pages' search engine performance or just add value for your visitors.

Generating a site map

A site map informs search engines which URLs on your site you want them to index. At a minimum, a site map consists of a list of the URLs on your site. It can also include when each URL was last updated, how often the URL changes, and how important it is in relation to other URLs in the site. This enables search engines to crawl the site more intelligently.

On some sites, not all pages are available through the human-browseable interface, that is, not all pages can be accessed by clicking on a link. If a human can't click on the link, then neither can the search engine crawler. On these sites, a site map is especially useful. The site map ensures that all pages will be crawled.

Using Magento, you can generate a site map containing all accessible URLs on your store's site. Then, you can instruct the search engines to index those URLs. Google, MSN, Yahoo, and Ask use the same protocol now.

 A site map increases the chance that all your pages will be included in search indexes. It does not influence the way that pages are ranked in search results.

In this section, we will cover generating a site map and pointing search engines towards the site map.

Getting ready

Before you can complete this task, you must have FTP access to your Magento site, that is, you must be able to upload, delete, and edit files in your Magento site.

How to do it...

1. Log in to your site's backend, or Administrative Panel.
2. Select **Catalog | Google Sitemap**.

 Although it's called a "Google Sitemap", the major search engines use the same protocol. So this site map will work for all of them.

3. Click on the **Add Sitemap** button. The **New Sitemap** page displays.
4. In the **Filename** field, enter a name for the site map.
5. In the **Path** field, enter the directory on your Magento server where you want the site map. To place it in the root (home) directory of your site, enter a forward slash like this: /
6. Click on the **Save & Generate** button, and the new site map is generated.
7. You can see a URL in the **Link for Google** column. Either copy and paste this URL into a document so that it can be easily retrieved, or minimize this window without closing it. Later, you will want to copy and paste this link.
8. Launch your FTP client, and navigate to the root directory of your Magento site:

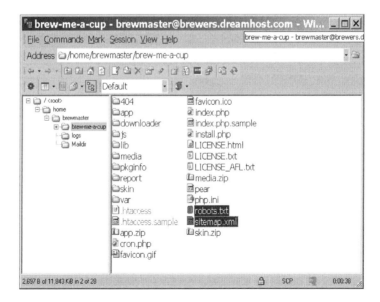

In our example, you can see the two files that we will deal with are in the root directory: **robots.txt** and **sitemap.xml**.

9. Open the file `robots.txt` for editing. Exactly how you do this depends upon which TP client you are using. If you are using WinSCP, as shown here, then you can just double-click on the file, and it will open for editing:

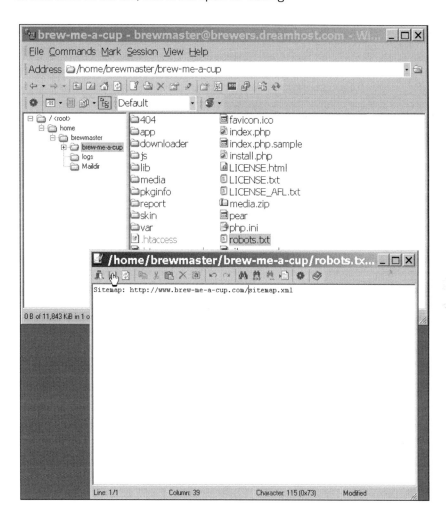

10. The file might already have some text in it. That's is okay. Add this line to the file:

   `Sitemap: http://www.yourdomain.com/sitemap.xml`

   where:

   `www.yourdomain.com` is your domain. In our example, it's
   `www.brew-me-a-cup.com`.

   `/sitemap.xml` is the path and filename for the site map. In our example, the site
   map is in the root directory. If we put Magento in a subdirectory, it might look like this:
   `www.brew-me-a-cup.com/magento/sitemap.xml`.

11. Save the file.

How it works...

When a search engine robot or crawler visits your site, the first file it looks for is `robots.txt`.
This file tells the crawler which pages to visit and which it should not visit. Robots are free to
abide by or ignore `robots.txt`. All of the major search engines will abide by `robots.txt`.
This ensures that they visit the pages you want them to index. It does not ensure that they will
actually index them or rank them higher.

There's more...

You can set up Magento to automatically refresh the site map file. This is the subject of the
next section *Configure Magento to automatically refresh the site map*.

Configuring Magento to automatically refresh the site map

After you set this up, you do not need to manually create the site map. Magento will create it
whenever you want.

Getting ready

Before you can complete this task, you must have FTP access to your Magento site, that is, you must be able to upload, delete, and edit files in your Magento site.

You must also be able to create **cron jobs** on your web server. Most hosting services enable you to create cron jobs. You should check the help files for your host, and ensure that you understand how to create a cron job.

Many hosting services offer the cPanel application for managing your files on the host. If your hosting service offers cPanel, then you might find this documentation helpful:

- The cPanel file manager:

  ```
  http://twiki.cpanel.net/twiki/bin/view/AllDocumentation/
  CpanelDocs/FileManager
  ```

- Creating a cron job in cPanel:

  ```
  http://twiki.cpanel.net/twiki/bin/view/AllDocumentation/
  CpanelDocs/CronJobs
  ```

How to do it...

Let's begin with creating the site map:

1. Log in to your site's backend or Administrative Panel.
2. Select **Catalog | Google Sitemap**.

 Although it's called a "Google Sitemap", the major search engines use the same protocol. So this site map will work for all of them.

3. Click on the **Add Sitemap** button. The **New Sitemap** page displays.
4. In the **Filename** field, enter a name for the site map.
5. In the **Path** field, enter the directory on your Magento server where you want the site map. To place it in the root (home) directory of your site, enter a slash like this: **/**
6. Click on the **Save & Generate** button, and the new site map is generated.
7. You can see a URL in the **Link for Google** column. Either copy and paste this URL into a document so that it can easily retrieve it, or minimize this window without closing it. Later, you will want to copy and paste this link.

Pointing search engine crawlers to the site map:

1. Launch your FTP client, and navigate to the root directory of your Magento site:

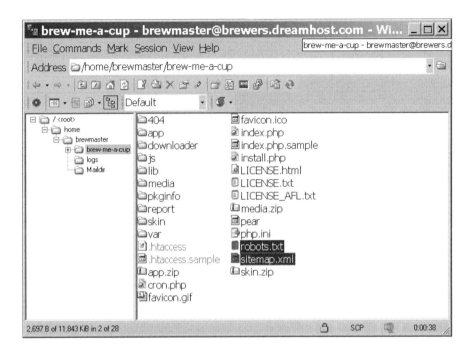

In our example, you can see the two files that we will deal with in the root directory: **robots.txt** and **sitemap.xml**.

2. Open the file `robots.txt` for editing. Exactly how you do this depends upon which FTP client you are using. If you are using WinSCP, as shown here, then you can just double-click on the file, and it will open for editing:

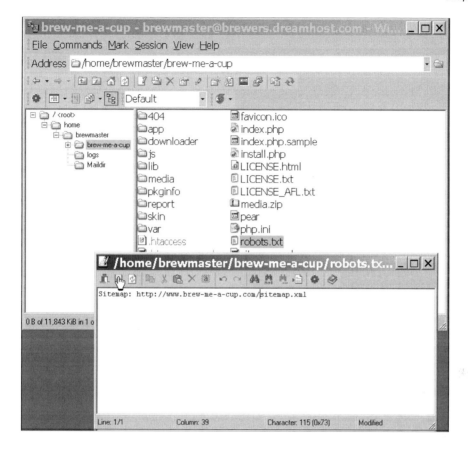

3. The file might already have some text in it. That's okay. Add this line to the file:

    `Sitemap: http://www.yourdomain.com/sitemap.xml`

    where:

    `www.yourdomain.com` is your domain. In our example, it's
    `www.brew-me-a-cup.com`.

    `/sitemap.xml` is the path and filename for the site map. In our example, the site
    map is in the root directory. If we put Magento in a subdirectory, it might look like this:
    `www.brew-me-a-cup.com/magento/sitemap.xml`.

4. Save the file.

Configuring Magento to periodically refresh the site map:

1. Log in to your site's backend or Administrative Panel.

2. Select **System | Configuration | Google Sitemap**.

3. Under **Categories Options**, **Products Options**, and **CMS Pages Options**, you will see a drop-down list labeled **Frequency**. This drop-down list answers the question, "How often do you update this kind of page in your store?"

   For example, if you add or edit products every day, then for **Products Options**, select a **Frequency** of **Daily**. If you add or edit category landing pages every week, then for **Categories Options**, select a **Frequency** of **Weekly**.

4. For **Categories Options**, **Products Options**, and **CMS Pages Options**, select the correct **Frequency** for your site.

5. Under **Categories Options**, **Products Options**, and **CMS Pages Options**, you will see a drop-down list labelled **Priority**. This drop-down list answers the question, "What is the relative importance of this kind of page?"

6. For example, if product pages are four times as important as category landing pages, then for **Products Options**, enter a **Priority** of **1.0**, and for **Categories Options**, enter a **Priority** of **0.25**.

7. For **Categories Options**, **Products Options**, and **CMS Pages Options**, enter the correct **Priority** for your site.

8. Under **Generation Settings**, select **Yes**. This turns on the feature. Magento will not generate the site map until you enable this.

9. Under **Start Time**, select the time you want the site map to be generated. On or after this time, Magento will generate your site map.

   For example, suppose you enter 2:30am here and your cron job is set to run every hour. When your cron job runs at 2:00am, it will not cause Magento to generate the site map. When the cron job runs again at 3:00am because the time for generating the site map has passed, Magento will generate the site map.

10. Under **Frequency**, select how often you want Magento to generate a site map. This can be **Daily**, **Weekly**, or **Monthly**. There is no point in generating a site map more often than once a day because a web crawler will almost certainly not visit your site any more often than that.

11. Under **Error Email Recipient**, enter the email address to which you want Magento to send errors. Magento will notify this email address if it encounters errors while trying to generate the sitemap.

12. The **Error Email Sender** is the email address from which the error email will appear to come. These email addresses are set up under **Store Email Addresses** on the same page.

13. The **Error Email Template** is the template that Magento will use when sending the error email. You can leave this at the default selection or create a new template under **System | Transactional Emails**.

14. Click on the **Save** button.

Setting up the Magento cron job:

On your web host, you must create a cron job. The cron job will tell the Magento script `cron.php` to execute a number of functions. Among those functions will be generating a new site map.

 Magento's `cron.php` is not the cron job. The cron job is script that you create on your web hosting service. The cron job, in turn, tells `cron.php` to run. The `cron.php` file then activates many functions, including generating a site map.

The method for creating a cron job will vary from host to host. In all cases, you want the cron job to run the file `cron.php`, found in Magento's home directory.

You should configure the cron job to run at least as often as you want the site map generated, that is, if you want a new site map generated daily, you should configure the cron job to run at least every day.

How it works...

Under **Catalog | Google Sitemap**, you told Magento what to call the site map and where to store it. In `robots.txt`, you told search engine crawlers where to find the site map.

Then, under **System | Configuration | Google Sitemap**, you told Magento how often to refresh the site map. You also chose some settings for the site map. These settings tell the search engine crawlers how often to check back for updated pages and the relative importance of different types of pages.

Finally, you created a cron job on your hosting service that runs `cron.php` at set times (every week, day, hour, and so on). The cron job runs `cron.php`, and `cron.php` tells Magento to refresh the site map.

2

Placing Products on Shopping Sites

In this chapter, you will learn how to place products on shopping sites. We will use Google Base as our example.

Placing products on shopping sites: One at a time

When shoppers want the best price possible for a product, they often use a shopping comparison site. Comparison sites such as www.nextag.com, www.pricegrabber.com, www.shopzilla.com, and Google shopping enable shoppers to find the best price and shipping rates. When the economy becomes more challenging, shoppers' use of comparison sites increases.

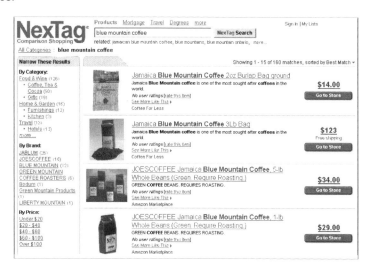

If you can offer the best combination of price, shipping rate, and service, then you should consider placing your products on these sites.

 In this section, we will use Google shopping as an example of a shopping comparison site. All of the major comparison sites work similarly.

The shopper's experience

Notice the results for Google product search are a mix of sponsored links (paid advertisements), and products submitted to Google:

Also, notice the **Show only** checkboxes near the upper left of the page. The shopper can show only those results that use Google Checkout, have free shipping, and that are new. Before placing your products on a comparison site, consider creating versions of the products that offer free shipping and that use Google Checkout. Then, when shoppers filter by these criteria, your products will be included in the results.

When a shopper clicks the link for a product, he/she is taken to the store offering that product. Hopefully, that will be your store.

Getting ready

Before you can complete this task, you must create a Google account. The easiest way to do this is by opening a Gmail account. Go to `www.gmail.com`, and sign up for an account.

The directions will assume that you have opened a Gmail account.

How to do it...

Let's begin with signing up for a Google Base account:

1. Log in to your Gmail account.

2. From the **more** menu, select **even more...**

3. A page of Google products displays. Scroll to the bottom of the page, and select **Business Solutions**.

4. Select the Google **Base: Product Search and more**.

5. The first time you select Google Base, you will see a link to **Sign in to Google Base**. Select this link.

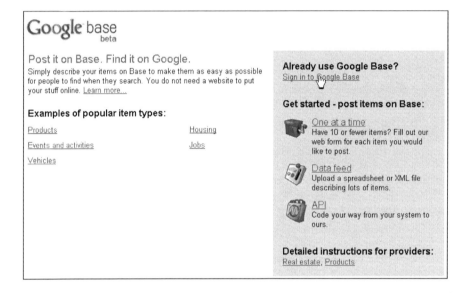

6. Enter and save your account information. This is a mix of information that shoppers will see and information that Google will use to contact you.

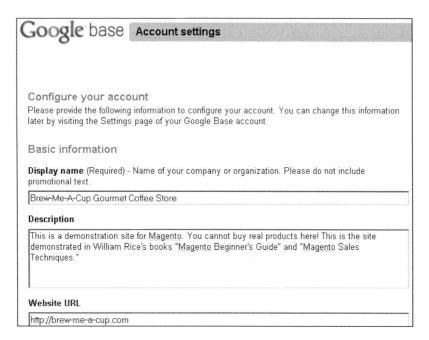

Adding items one at a time:

1. Log in to your Google Base account. You can do this by logging in to your Gmail account and navigating to Google Base, as shown above, or go to `http://google.com/base` and log in.

2. Under the **My Items** tab, select the **Active items** subtab.

3. Select the **Add an item** button.

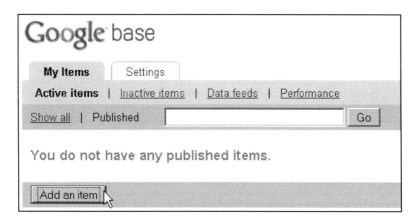

4. On the resulting page, from the **Choose an existing item type** drop-down list, select **Products**.

5. Select the **Next** button.
6. On the **edit item** page, enter details for this product.

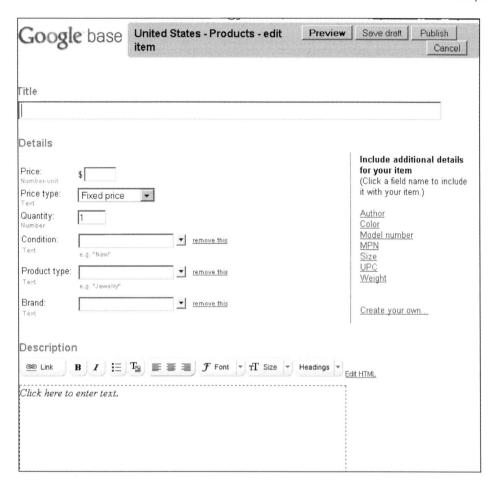

7. For the **Title**, enter the name of the product that you want shoppers to see when they are searching for the product.

8. For **Price**, enter the price that you want shoppers to see when the product is listed.

9. The **Quantity** is the number that you have in your inventory, not the number that the shopper is buying. Note that Google will not update this number when you sell one through your store. As long as you set a number above zero, Google Base will display your item.

10. Either select a **Condition**, or if it's not relevant, click on **remove this** to remove the field from the product listing.

11. For **Product type**, you can click on the drop-down arrow, and select one of the values presented, or type in a product type.

12. Continue for the rest of the fields, until you reach **Description**.

13. To remove a field, click on **remove this**.

14. To add a field from the list on the right, click on its name.

15. To create a new field, click on **Create your own...** and fill in the resulting fields.

16. Scroll down to the **Description** field. The easiest way to add a description might be to copy and paste it from your Magento product page.

17. Edit the remaining fields, if needed. These will be the **Contact** and **Payment** fields.

18. **Preview** your listing to ensure it is correct.

19. From the preview screen, either **Edit** or **Publish** your item.

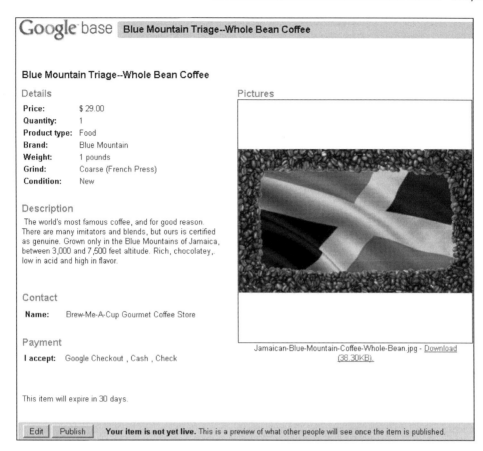

20. After you publish the item, it will appear in your list of active items.

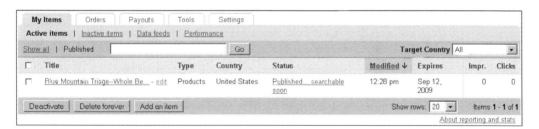

How it works...

Google Base enables you to submit items, other than web pages, to Google's search engine: events, jobs, products, and more. Products submitted through Google Base will be indexed in their Product Search.

You are submitting individual products, not product pages. A product that you submit to Google Base can link through to the product page in your Magento store, or it can link to a completely different site.

Google's normal web search can still index your product pages. Optimizing your product pages for web searches has been covered in chapter 4, *Making the Sale by Optimizing Product Pages*.

Uploading products to Google Base

The previous section showed you how to submit one product to Google Base. If you have 10 or fewer products to submit, then that method is probably the fastest. If you have more than 10 products to submit, then you might want to expend the extra effort of uploading them all at once.

Getting ready

Before you try to upload multiple products, you should go through the aforementioned procedure for placing a single product on a shopping site. Doing that first will ensure that you have opened the required Google account and that you understand the structure of Google Product Search.

 Before trying this procedure, complete the previous procedure at least once.

How to do it...

After logging in to Google Base, you will need to map product attributes from Magento to Google Base. This ensures that Magento's price shows up in Google's price, Magento's description shows up in Google's description, and so on. Then, you will upload the products.

Let's begin with entering your Google Base credentials into Magento:

1. Log in to the Magento admin interface.
2. Select **System | Configuration**.
3. On the **Configuration** page, under the **Sales** section, select **Google API**.
4. On the **Google API** page, select the **Google Base** section.
5. Enter your login information for Google Base.
6. Save the configuration.

Mapping product attributes from Magento to Google Base:

1. Sign in to your Google Base account.

2. Select **My Items | Data Feeds | Learn more about data feeds**.

3. Select the tab **Select Item Type**.

4. Under **Popular Item Types**, select **Products**.

5. Scroll down the page until you see a section labeled **Attributes**. Under that section, you will see a list of the required attributes that you must include for each product:

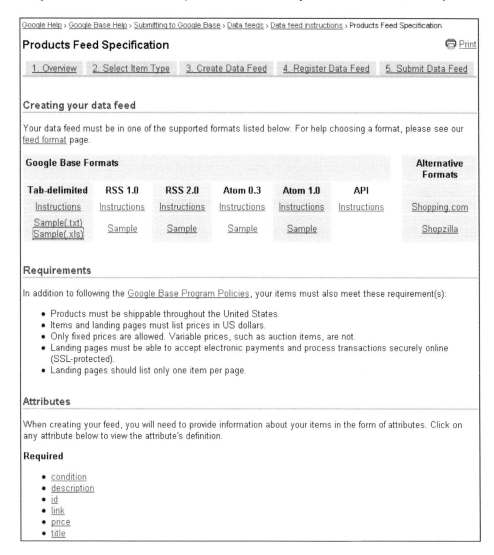

Scrolling further down the page shows you the recommended and optional attributes.

When you extract the list of products from Magento, you will need to match the product attributes in Magento to the attributes in Google Base. Magento has a tool to help you do that.

6. Keep this window (or tab) open in your browser. You will use it for reference later on.

7. In a new browser window or tab, log in to the Magento admin interface.

8. Select **Catalog | Google Base | Manage Attributes**.

9. Click on the button for **Add Attribute Mapping**. A section appears in the window labeled **Attribute Set** and **Google Base Item Type**.

10. For **Target Country**, select the country in which you want to sell the products.

11. For **Attribute Set**, select the Magento attribute set that you used for the products. If your store uses several attribute sets, you will need to do this process for each one of them.

12. For **Google Base Item Type**, you will probably select **products**. Now the **Attributes Mapping** section, would have the **Add New Attribute** button on it.

13. Click on the **Add New Attribute** button. A new line appears in the **Attributes Mapping** section.

Where are all the attributes? Some of them are missing!

At this point, you will begin mapping Magento attributes to Google Base attributes. You might notice that attributes required by Google Base are not listed here. That is because Magento has already mapped those attributes for you. That part is built into Magento's functions. Here, you are mapping just the optional attributes.

14. From the left drop-down list, select the Magento attribute that you want to include for the products:

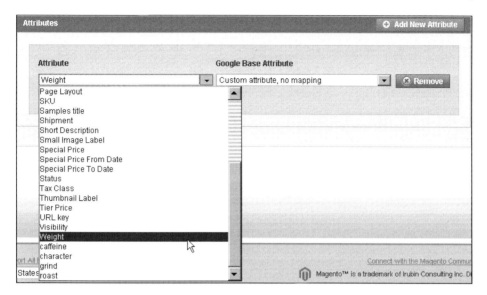

15. From the right drop-down list, select the **Google Base Attribute** that matches the Magento attribute:

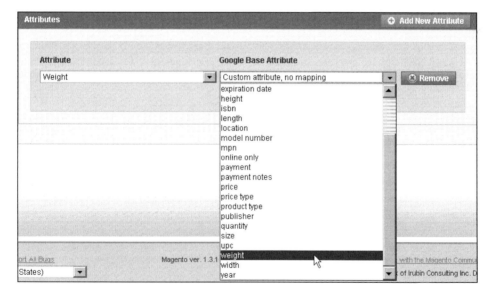

16. Continue adding new attributes as needed.

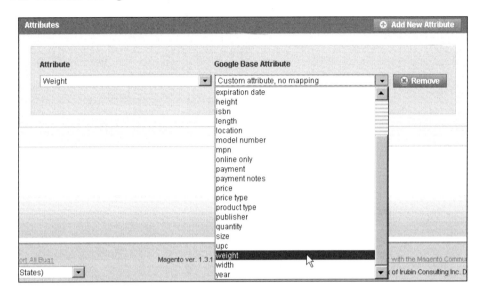

17. When you finish the map, select **Save Mapping**.

 Be sure that you understand what information the Magento attribute holds. For example, cost doesn't hold the price that you charge the customer; it holds your cost for the product. And if you're unsure what information a Google Base Attribute should hold, then switch back to the Google Base web page that you opened earlier and read the description for the attribute.

Selecting and adding products to Google Base:

1. Select **Catalog | Google Base | Manage Items**.

   The top part of the page displays items that you have put into Google Base. If this is the first time you have used this page, then that section will be blank. The bottom part of the page shows all items available that you can include in Google Base. Because you have not searched for any items yet, that part is also blank.

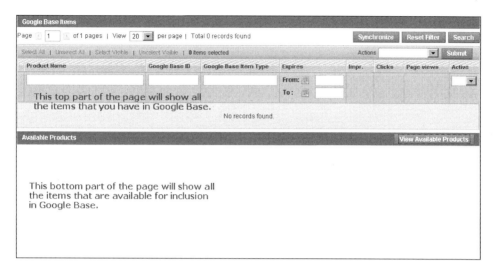

2. Select the button **View Available Products**, and all the products in your catalog will be listed.

3. From the **Attrib. Set Name** drop-down list, select the attribute set for the products that you want to put onto Google Base. Ideally, you should have created a mapping for that attribute set.

4. In the same shaded row where you selected the attribute set, you can enter other search criteria. If needed, narrow your search by **ID**, **Product Name**, **SKU**, and **Price**.

5. Click on the **Search** button.

   Only the products that meet the search criteria will be displayed. In our example, notice that we searched for products that use the **coffee-by-pound** attribute set. In the search results, you can see that all of the products listed use that attribute set.

6. From the search results, select the products that you want to add to Google Base. You can select them one at a time, or use the links across the top of the section: **Select All**, **Unselect All**, **Select Visible**, and **Unselect Visible**.

7. From the **Actions** drop-down list, select **Add to Google Base**.

8. Click on the **Submit** button. The selected items will be added to Google Base. They will also be displayed in the top part of the page.

How it works...

Magento links directly to your Google Base account and uploads products from its catalog into Google Base. The attributes that Google Base requires should always be programmed into the latest version of Magento. If you experience errors because of field mappings, then check the Magento forums to see if it's because you are not running the latest version and if there is a workaround.

3
Driving Visitors to Your Product Pages

When shoppers land at your store, you want them to stay and shop. You can encourage them to explore your product pages using landing pages. A **landing page** is a visitor's first impression of your store. Ideally, you want the landing page to drive the visitor to one of your product pages.

Closely related to landing pages are "About" pages. These pages tell the visitor about your store. They can include a contact page, privacy notice, billing practices, company history, and more. These pages can reassure visitors about your business practices and make your store appear more legitimate.

Landing pages and about pages are related because you use the same tool to create them: Magento's CMS pages. Therefore, in this chapter, you will learn how to:

- ▶ Customize Magento's default CMS pages
- ▶ Create new CMS pages
- ▶ Decide which About pages to include
- ▶ Decide what content to include on About pages

Introduction

A landing page is not a product page. On a landing page, the visitor doesn't select the color of a product, leave a rating, or add something to the shopping cart. Instead, the landing page delivers a message or encourages the visitor to take some action.

A landing page is often matched to a specific advertisement. For example, suppose we place an ad for our coffee store on a coffee lover's site. In the following screenshot, notice the ad in the lower-right corner:

Clicking that ad takes the visitor to a landing page in our store:

Notice that the graphic and text on this landing page complement the graphic and text in the ad. There is an art and science to creating online ads and their landing pages. You can find many books and online resources for this. For example, searching for "landing page optimization" and "creating landing pages" will produce many results.

A complete discussion of landing page optimization is far beyond the scope of this book. Instead, we will focus on the process of creating landing pages.

The top part of this landing page, above the product listing, is a basic landing page. It consists of basic HTML code. We will see how to create that part of the page first.

The bottom part of this landing page consists of a dynamic display of the products mentioned on the page. This is accomplished by inserting some more advanced HTML code into the page and choosing some settings in the admin interface. We will see how to create that part of the page later.

Creating a basic landing page

This procedure will show you how to create a basic landing page with static text. In Magento, we call this a **CMS** page. The page will look like the following:

Getting ready

Before you begin creating a landing page like the previous image, you should:

1. Prepare any graphics used in the page.

2. Be prepared to upload the graphics to your site.

3. Note any links that you want to include on the page.

4. Write the text for the page. A plain text editor will work fine.

5. Decide the URL you want for the page. In our example, we used `http://brew-me-a-cup.com/gourmet-coffee-in-bed`.

6. Point your online ad to the URL for the landing page.

How to do it...

Let's begin by uploading the graphics to your site:

1. Launch your FTP application, and point it at your Magento site.

2. Navigate to the /media directory.

3. Upload the graphics to the /media directory.

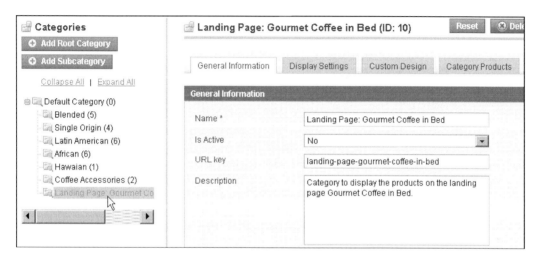

Creating the page:

1. Log in to your site's backend or Admin Panel.

2. Select **CMS | Manage Pages**. The **Manage Pages** page displays. A list of the CMS pages (or "static pages") in your store should appear on this page.

3. Click on the **Add New Page** button. The **Edit Page** will display. The **General Information** tab is selected for you.

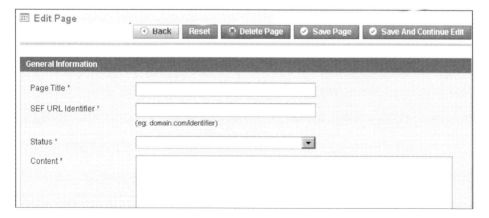

4. Enter a **Page Title**. This will appear in the title bar of the visitor's browser.

5. Enter an **SEF URL Identifier**. This will be added to your domain name to form the URL of the page. For example, we entered gourmet-coffee-in-bed, so the URL of our page will be `http://brew-me-a-cup.com/gourmet-coffee-in-bed`.

6. To activate this page, under **Status** select **Enabled**.

7. In the **Content** field, enter the HTML code for this page.

   For example, we entered this HTML code:

   ```
   <img src="http://brew-me-a-cup.com/media/Would you serve her
   bad coffee 2.png" alt="Woman Drinking Gourmet Coffee in Bed"
   height=400 width=266 />
   ```

   Our **Edit Page** looked like this:

   And the resulting CMS page displayed this in the visitor's browser:

Obviously, we need more on this page than just a graphic. Let's continue creating the page.

8. Add the rest of the HTML code to the CMS page. Save and preview the page frequently to ensure that you are creating the page you want.

    For example, we entered the following HTML code:

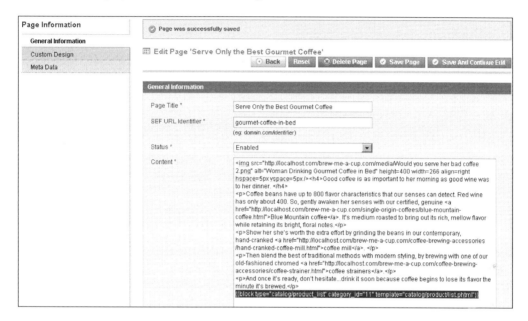

The resultant page looks like the following:

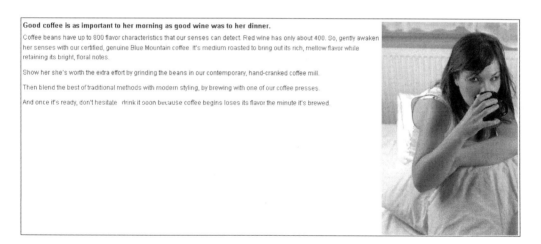

Applying a layout template to the CMS page:

Our HTML code appears to be working fine. However, notice that this page is missing all of the other features that we normally have on our Magento pages. There is no header, footer, menu bar across the top, color scheme, search box, and so on. We need to perform an additional step to get these features.

1. Select the **Custom Design** tab.

2. If you are using a custom theme, then from the **Custom Theme** drop-down list, select the name of that theme.

3. From the **Layout** drop-down list, select the type of layout that you want for this static page. In our example, we selected **2 columns with left bar**.

4. Save and preview. You should see that a Magento template has been applied to the CMS page. The content (HTML code) that you entered appears on a Magento page. You now have a basic landing page.

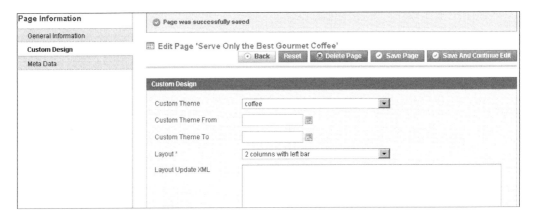

How it works...

Anything that can be put on a web page using HTML can be put onto your CMS pages. These CMS pages can be completely standalone or they can have a Magento layout template applied to them.

There's more...

The basic CMS page that we created in this procedure is static. It does not have any dynamic content. That is, it does not have any content that is generated at the time the page is viewed.

You can make the page dynamic by adding a Magento block to the page. In the next section, you will see how to add products to the page using a block. That block will display the products mentioned on the page. In the following example, we have added products to the simple landing page that we just created:

Adding a products block to a landing page

In the preceding example, we added products to a simple landing page. To do this, we:

1. Created a product category just for that landing page.

2. Added the three products that you see to that category.

3. Added a block to the page that displays all of the products in that category.

Each of these is covered in a subsection below. You can add other blocks to a Magento CMS page. For example, the **Search** and **Related Products** blocks. We will use the **Category Product** block as our example.

How to do it...

Creating a product category for the landing page:

1. Log in to your site's administrative interface.

2. Select **Catalog | Manage Categories**.

3. Under the **Default** category, add a new subcategory.

4. For the category **Name**, you might want to include the words "Landing Page" or something similar. When you are assigning products to this category, you will see this name.

5. For **Is Active**, select **No**. This will prevent the category from being displayed in the navigation menu. Remember, you want to use this category only on a landing page. You do not want it to appear in your navigation menus.

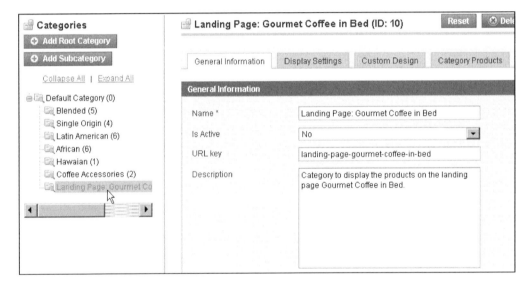

6. The **URL** key does not matter. This category will not have its own page. It will always be embedded on a landing page. So, the URL for the products in this category will be the URL of the landing page.

7. You can make the **Description** something that will help you remember the purpose of this category.

8. You can skip the rest of the fields and tabs in this category. Save the category.

9. In the title bar, take note of the category ID. Write it down, as you will need it later.

Adding products to the landing page category:

1. Select **Catalog | Manage Products** The **Manage Products** page displays. A list of the products in your store should appear on this page.

2. For the product that you want to appear on the landing page, select the **Edit** link. The **Product Information** page displays. The **General** tab will be selected for you.

3. Select the **Categories** tab.

4. From the list of product categories, select the category that you created for your landing page. Because the category is not active, it should be grayed out.

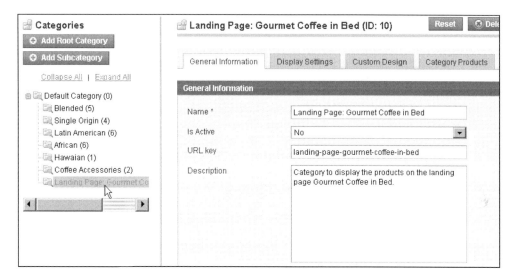

5. Save the product.

6. Repeat this for each product that you want to appear on the landing page.

Adding the landing page category to the landing page:

1. Select **CMS | Manage Pages**. The **Manage Pages** page displays. A list of the CMS pages (or "static pages") in your store should appear on this page.

2. From the list of pages, select the landing page.

3. When the page displays, the **General Information** tab should be selected. Click to place the insertion point into the **Content** field.

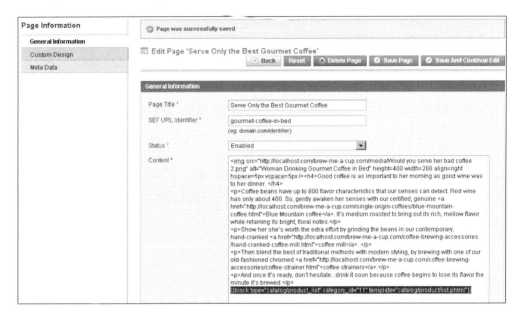

4. Enter the code that will display the category product block on that page. In our example, the code is:

```
{{block type="catalog/product_list" category_id="11"
template="catalog/product/list.phtml"}}
```

where:

block places a block on the page.

type is the type of block. The type of block determines what it does.

category_id is the ID number of the product category.

template is the HTML code that determines the layout of the block. The template determines how it looks.

5. Save and preview. You should see that the block has been added to the page.

How it works...

The landing page that we created in this procedure works in almost the same way as a normal category page. Remember that both the landing page with the category product block and a category display page, display products from the selected category.

So, what is the difference between this landing page and a normal category page? The most important difference is that the product category used on this landing page has the setting **Is Active** set to **No**, so that it will not appear in the navigation menu on the left side of the page or across the top of the page. A normal category is usually active because you want it to show up in the categories menu.

There's more...

To create the landing page in this exercise, we used the static pages feature. A static page can be a landing page, a page giving information about your store, or a page of helpful techniques on how to best enjoy your products, as well as many other things.

Ideas for static pages

This section describes some ideas for static pages. Some of these, such as the About pages, are part of almost every legitimate online store. Others are fun ideas that can draw traffic to your store. Wherever possible, include links to your categories or products in these pages.

Fun pages

If a fun page is shared by people who like it, then it can become highly ranked in search engines. This helps to bring visitors to your site.

If you're selling products made in an exotic country, then educate and intrigue your reader by educating them about the exoticness of the country. Tie it back to your products by mentioning how your products reflect the exotic and unique character of that place.

You can search video sharing sites, such as `www.youtube.com`, for funny videos that have your type of product in them. For example, our demonstration store sells coffee. A search for funny coffee videos yields a video clip from the classic Charlie Chaplin film, *Modern Times*.

You can embed this video on one of your static pages by copying the Embed HTML code from the YouTube page and pasting it into your static page. You can place several videos on a page.

Informative pages

Static pages offer you the opportunity to teach visitors about your field. Don't teach them about your products because that's what product pages are for. Instead, teach them about the business and tie it back to your products.

You can create a static page to show your customers how your products are made. For example, if you're selling coffee or wine, teach them how it's all made from the same species of bean or grape, and that what differs is the territory, treatment, and processing. Maybe describe the different wine growing regions and link to some products from each region.

If your products require some skill to use, then you can create pages showing them how to use your products. Our example store might benefit from a static page teaching visitors about the different types of coffee grinds and a link to our coffee grinder.

 Notice that in both of the preceding examples, we link from the informative page to some products. If the informative page becomes a popular destination because of the information it contains, then it can help to drive visitors to our product pages.

About pages

You can use static pages to tell visitors about your business. Magento has some static pages built in for this purpose. By default, the **About Us** and **Customer Service** pages appear in links in the footer of your store.

About Us | Customer Service
Site Map | Search Terms | Advanced Search | Contact Us

Help Us to Keep Magento Healthy - **Report All Bugs** (ver. 1.3.2.1)
© 2008 William Rice Inc. All Rights Reserved.

In Magento's default installation, these pages contain dummy text:

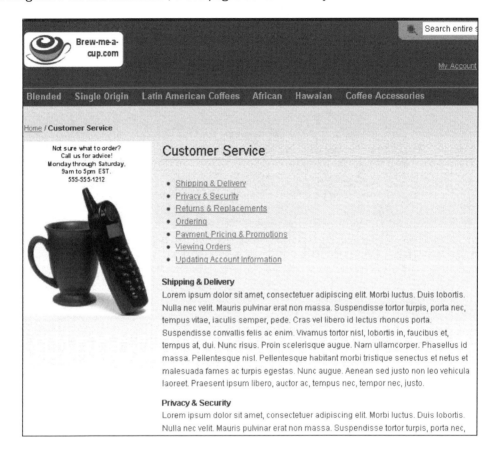

 You should customize the content of the **About Us** and **Customer Service** pages under **CMS | Manage Pages**.

The About Us page

One of the most important things your **About Us** page can do is give your business legitimacy. Here is a list of some items that you can include on your **About Us** page:

- ▶ Official, registered business name, corporation name, and corporation registration.

- ▶ Your company history, if it adds credibility. Before opening your online store, were you a brick-and-mortar business for 20 years?

- ▶ Your company mission statement.

- ▶ Recent company news and awards. Stress recent, or this gives the impression that you've abandoned your store.

- ▶ A prominent link to the **Contact Us** page.

- ▶ Photos of physical assets and people such as delivery vans, warehouse, employees, and equipment.

- ▶ A list and explanation of industry memberships and credentials or a prominent link to a memberships and awards page. Consider membership in these organisations:

  - ❑ TRUSTe www.truste.org.

  - ❑ Shopsafe www.shopsafe.co.uk,www.shopsafe.com

  - ❑ TrustedShops www.trustedshops.com and www.trustedshops.de

  - ❑ eBay PowerSeller

  - ❑ SafeBuy www.safebuy.org.uk

  - ❑ buySAFE www.buysafe.com

  - ❑ BBBonline www.bbbonline.org

Note that the About page is one of the least visited in most shopping sites. So, while you may put explanations for your credentials on this page, consider putting the graphic (the "badge" or "seal") for that credential in a more prominent place such as the footer or a static block.

All of these items can reassure customers that you are a legitimate business.

The Customer Service page

The default **Customer Service** page that comes with Magento contains these sections:

- **Shipping & Delivery**
- **Privacy & Security**
- **Returns & Replacements**
- **Ordering**
- **Payment**, **Pricing & Promotions**
- **Viewing Orders**
- **Updating Account Information**

Some stores would place these on separate pages. You can do that by creating separate static pages for each of them. Whether you keep them on the same page or separate them, you should update Magento's default **Customer Service** page.

 In some jurisdictions, you might be required by law to publish your Terms and Conditions, Privacy Policy, Billing Policy, and Shipping Policy on your website. Check your local laws to ensure that you are publishing all of the information required of you.

Writing your own store policies can take a lot of time. Hiring a lawyer to write them for you can take a lot of money. There are vendors (many of them lawyers) who sell verbiage that you can use for your store policies. Conduct a web search using the keywords "e-commerce terms and conditions document".

4
Making the Sale by Optimizing Product Pages

When shoppers land on a product page, you want that page to present the product in the best possible way. The product page should entice, inform, and entertain your shoppers.

There are several things you can do to optimize product pages for selling. In this chapter, we will look at these techniques:

- ▶ Add custom options
- ▶ Add videos, links, and other HTML to product pages
- ▶ Optimize product images
- ▶ Tell a story using product images
- ▶ Change the layout of a product page

Adding custom options

In Magento, a custom option is a field that enables your customer to specify something that he/she wants customized. For example, suppose you sell sports trophies that can be engraved with the name of the event and the winning team then you would add a custom option to that product, where the shopper enters the text to engrave. If you offer a style of shirt in different sizes and each size is a different product with its own stock number, then that is a configurable product. If you offer a style of shirt that is custom-made on demand, and the customer chooses the measurements for that shirt (chest size, sleeve length, neck size, and so on), then that is a simple product with custom options.

In the following example, the customer can add his/her initials as a custom option. Selecting any of the options adds a product, with its own SKU, to the customer's order.

How to do it...

Let's begin with adding the custom option:

1. Log in to your site's backend or Administrative Panel.

2. Select **Catalog | Manage Products**. The **Manage Products** page displays. You will see a list of the products in your store.

3. For the product that you want, select the **Edit** link. The **Product Information** page displays. The **General** tab will be selected for you.

4. Select the **Custom Options** tab.

5. Click the **Add New Option** button. A new option appears. You will need to fill in the fields to complete this option.

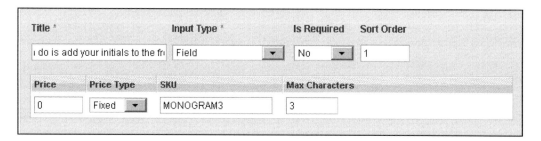

6. In the **Title** field, add text that will appear next to the option. The text that you see in the example above, "This is an expensive machine..." and "Extra filter cups...", was entered into the **Title** field.

Selecting the input type:

1. Select the input type for this option. Based upon the type you select, other fields will appear. You will be required to fill in these other fields.

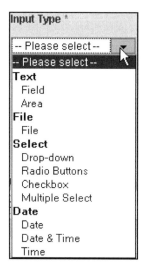

If you select this Input type...	You will also need to specify...
Text	The maximum number of characters the shopper can enter into the text field or text area.

If you select this Input type...	You will also need to specify...
FIle	The filename extensions that you will allow the shopper to upload. For example, you might supply the shopper with a detailed form to fill out using Adobe Acrobat Reader and then have them upload the form. In that case, you would specify `.pdf` as the filename extension.
Select	Each of the selections that they can make. You add selections by clicking on the **Add New Row** button.
Date	Nothing. This just adds a field where the shopper enters a date and/or time.

Selecting the remaining options:

1. The **Is Required** drop-down menu determines if the customer must select this custom option to order the product. For example, if you're selling custom-made shirts, then you might require the customer to enter measurements into the custom option fields.

2. The **Sort Order** field determines the order in which the custom options are displayed. They appear from lowest to highest.

3. The **Price** is a required field. If you set it to zero, then no price will display.

4. **Price Type** is **Fixed** if you always charge the same for that option. Setting it to **Percent** calculates the price for the option based on the price for the product.

5. **SKU** is not required, but if the option is another product (like extra parts), then you will want to use it.

6. Save the product, and preview it in your store.

How it works...

Both custom options and configurable products give your customer a choice. But they are not the same. When a customer chooses a configurable product, the customer is ordering a separate product with its own stock number, price, and inventory. When a customer chooses a custom option, the customer is not choosing a different product. Instead, the customer is choosing an additional feature or part for the product. These custom additions can be free or they can have their own price. Each custom option has its own SKU number.

There's more...

You can get especially creative with the custom option that allows customers to upload files. For example, you can:

- ▸ Enable customers to upload a graphic that you add to the product, such as a graphic that is silkscreened on a laptop's case.

- ▸ Sell a picture printing and framing service. The customer uploads a digital picture, and you print it on high-quality photographic paper and frame it.

- ▸ Supply customers with a detailed form for specifying a product, and then have the customer upload the form as part of their order.

- ▸ Run a contest for the best picture of a customer using a product. Customers upload the picture under the product. You then add the best pictures to a static page on your site.

Adding videos, links, and other HTML to product pages

You enter the description for a product on the product page under the **General** tab:

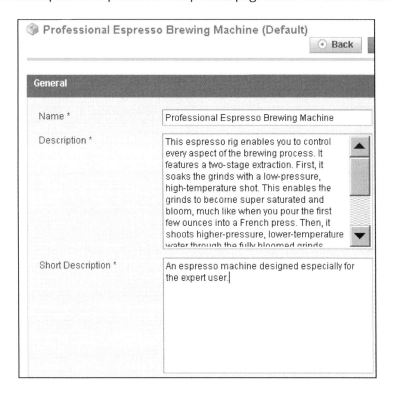

While these fields appear to accept only text, they will accept HTML code. This means that you can add almost anything to the product description that you can add to a standard web page. For example, let's embed a video into the **Short Description** field.

How to do it...

1. Navigate to the video site that contains the video you want to embed. In our example, we're embedding a video from YouTube:

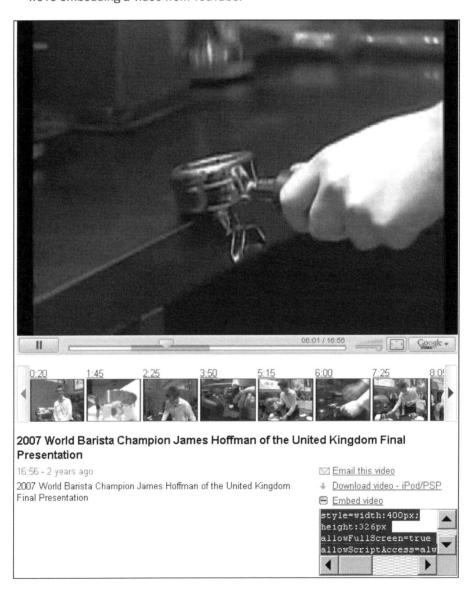

2. Clicking on the **Embed video** link selects the code that we need to put on our product page.

3. Select and copy the code.

4. Log in to Magento's backend, and go to the **Product Information** page, **General** tab.

5. Paste the copied code into either of the description fields.

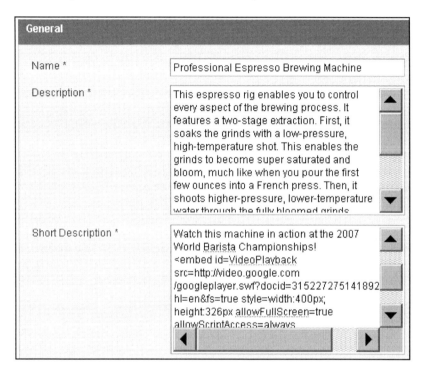

6. Save the product.

How it works...

The HTML code that you enter into the description field is displayed when the customer views the product. Any valid HTML code will work. In our example, we embedded the video in the **Short Description** field, which placed it near the top of the page, under **Quick Overview**:

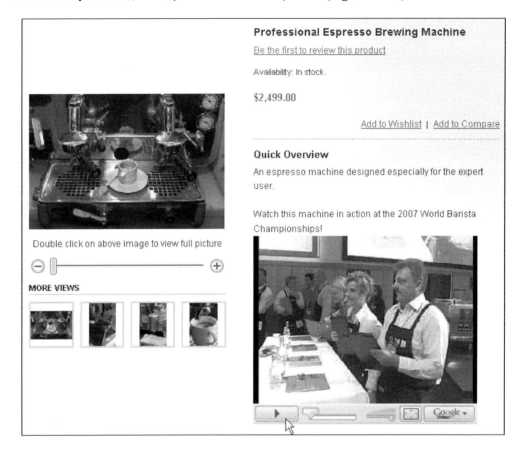

There's more...

Using HTML, you can:

- ▸ Embed videos in your product page
- ▸ Add links to your product page
- ▸ Add the manufacturer's graphic to the product description

Just remain aware of how much space the Magento layout gives you for the items that you want to put on the page. For example, the code that we copied from www.youtube.com above makes the video 400 pixels wide which is too wide for our Magento page, so we had to change it to 300 pixels.

Optimizing product images

The default Magento template uses three sizes of pictures: **Base Image**, **Small Image**, and **Thumbnail**. These are uploaded on the **Product Information** page under the **Images** tab. Magento uses these different sizes in different places:

Size	Pixels	Where it's Used
Base	265 x 265 (or larger)	On the product page
Small	135 x 135	In catalog listings
Thumbnail	75 x 75	On the checkout page

The easiest thing to do is upload a large, square product picture and let Magento generate the other sizes. However, this doesn't always give the best results. At small sizes, your product might not be recognizable. Consider this catalog page, where the product images appear at a size of 135 x 135 pixels. The following page is at the actual size:

At the small size, these products might not be immediately recognized by a shopper. If you're using the default template, you would need to change the template files to change the default picture sizes. However, you can crop and zoom the images to make your products more recognizable and appealing at the default size. Notice the following image of the coffee press pot:

Once our shopper is on the product page, Magento displays the base image at 265 x 265 pixels. If you've uploaded an image larger than that, then Magento also enables the shopper to display a larger size. In the following screenshot, you can see that the shopper has double-clicked on the product image, and Magento now displays the product at its maximum size:

Getting ready

Before you begin, you should:

- ▸ Have at least one large graphic for the product.
- ▸ Have a graphics program that enables you to crop and resize graphics.

How to do it...

Let's begin by checking the size of your catalog listing graphics:

1. Navigate to your site, and display one of the catalog pages. A category home page is usually a good choice. You want to view any product listing like this:

2. Right-click on one of the product images. From the pop-up menu, select **Properties**.

3. The **Element Properties** window will display. Take note of the image dimensions. For the default Magento installation, these are 135 x 135 pixels. Yours might differ. If they do, then for the rest of these instructions, use the dimensions for your site.

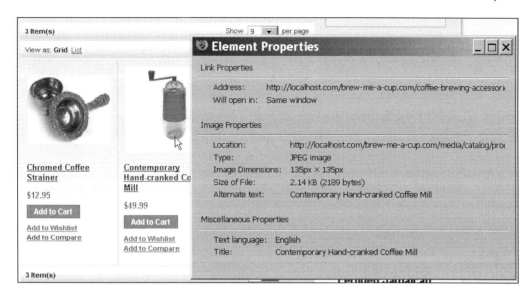

4. Close the **Properties** window.

Now, let's crop and size the small product image:

1. In your favorite graphics editor, open the product image.

2. Decide which part of the image is most visually compelling for a potential shopper.

Question	Example
Is a part of this image visually striking? Especially beautiful? Surprising? Or provocative? For example, these eyeglasses have a distinctive shape on their outer rims, and a striking color on their earpieces.	

Question	Example
Does a part of this image show something that I know my shoppers want? For example, this multi-tool for snowboarders has a bit that enables you to unscrew and adjust snowboard bindings. For a snowboarder, this bit is the most important part of the product.	
Does a part of this image make the product instantly recognizable? In this example, if you display the image at a size of 135 x 135 pixels, the blood pressure cuff will be so small that you cannot recognize it. In the catalog listing, you will probably want to display the cuff large enough so that shoppers can see the markings on the cuff. If a shopper can read the SYS, DIA, and Pulse that are printed on the cuff, he/she will probably recognize it instantly as a blood pressure device.	

3. Using your graphic application's cropping tool, select the area of the image that you decided upon in the previous step. Remember, this will be displayed at 135 x 135 pixels. You don't need to make your selection 135 pixels because you can resize it. However, you should try to make the selection as square as possible.

4. In the previous screenshot, notice that Paint Shop Pro tells us the selection is 208 x 208 pixels. When we upload this to Magento, and select it as the small size image, Magento will generate a graphic that is 135 x 135 pixels.

5. Save the graphic as a .jpg or .png file.

Uploading the image to Magento:

1. Log in to your site's backend or Admin Panel.

2. Select **Catalog | Manage Products**. The **Manage Products** page displays. You will see a list of the products in your store.

3. For the product that you want, select the **Edit** link. The **Product Information** page displays. The **General** tab will be selected for you.

4. Select the **Images** tab.

5. Select the **Browse Images...** button.

6. A dialog box pops up. Navigate to where you saved the small graphic, and select the file.

7. In the dialog box, click the **Open** or **OK** button.
8. You will be returned to the **Images** page. Click the **Upload Files** button.
9. After the file uploads, roll over it to display the image. Make sure this is the image that you intended.
10. Next to the image, select the radio button for **Small Image**.

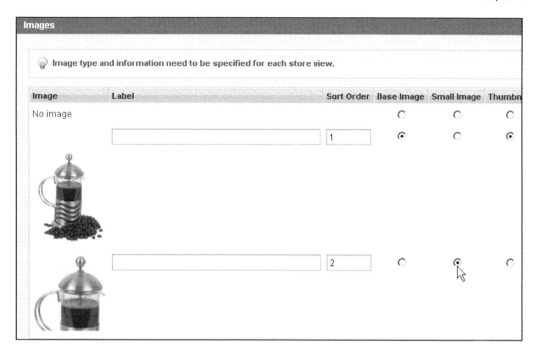

11. Save the product.

Do you want customers to see this image on the product page? By default, all of the images that you upload to the **Images** tab can be seen on the product page. Remember that you uploaded this image so that you can use it in catalog listings. If the image that you uploaded is smaller than 265 x 265, then you might want to exclude it from the product page. To prevent this image from displaying on the product page, so that it is used only in the product listings, click on the **Exclude** checkbox and save the product.

How it works...

Whenever Magento displays this product in the product listings (such as a category home page or product comparisons), the optimized image that you just uploaded will be used.

Telling a story with product images

Magento enables you to assign multiple images to a product. On the product page, these images are displayed under **MORE VIEWS**. In the following screenshot, you can see that the coffee press has a main image and an additional image:

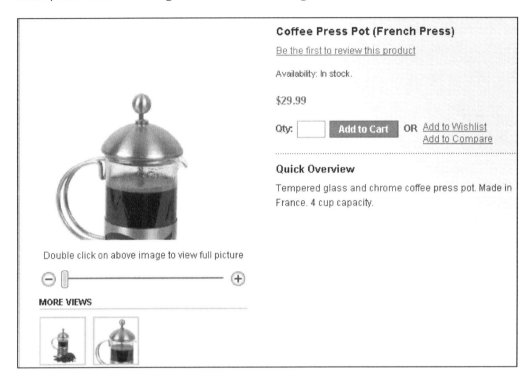

When a shopper double-clicks the main image, or clicks an image under **MORE VIEWS**, a pop-up window displays the image. Notice that the window has a **Next >>** link, which takes the shopper to the next image:

Giving your shoppers multiple images for a product is almost always good. Telling a story with those images can be even better. To tell a story with product images, you will need to:

1. Create multiple images that are designed to tell a story.
2. Upload the images to Magento.
3. Tell Magento the order in which to display the images.
4. Add a title for each image.

Each of these is covered in the following section:

How to do it...

Let's begin by creating images designed to tell a story. Create a series of images that tell a story about using the product. For example, if we're selling an espresso machine, we might create this series of images:

Notice that the series contains an image of the complete product. Moreover, each image features an important part of the product. In some of the images, we see a person using the product. In all except the complete product, we see something happening; they are action shots. Consider these principles when you design your series of images: complete product, important features, people, and action.

Because these images will be displayed on the product page, they can be large in size. Make them at least 265 x 265 pixels. If they are larger, then shoppers will be able to zoom in and scroll the pictures.

Uploading the images to Magento:

1. Log in to your site's backend or Admin Panel.

2. Select **Catalog | Manage Products**. The **Manage Products** page displays. You will see a list of the products in your store.

3. For the product that you want, select the **Edit** link. The **Product Information** page displays. The General tab will be selected for you.

4. Select the **Images** tab.

5. Select the **Browse Images...** button.

6. A dialog box pops up. Navigate to where you saved the graphics, and select the first graphic.

7. In the dialog box, click the **Open** or **OK** button.

8. You will be returned to the **Images** page. The graphic file that you selected will be listed at the bottom of the page.

9. For each graphic, repeat steps 5 through 7, until you have selected all of the graphics in the sequence.

10. Click the **Upload Files** button.

11. The graphics will be uploaded to Magento. Roll over each one to preview the graphic.

Tell Magento the order in which to display the images:

1. In the **Sort Order** column, enter a number that indicates the order in which Magento should display the images.

2. Select the **Save and Continue Edit** button.

Adding a title for each image:

1. In the **Label** column, enter a label, or caption, for each graphic. This label will appear in the title of the graphic window.

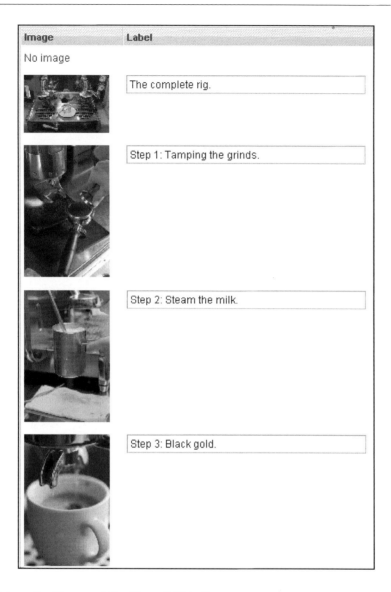

Image	Label
No image	
	The complete rig.
	Step 1: Tamping the grinds.
	Step 2: Steam the milk.
	Step 3: Black gold.

2. Click on the **Save and Continue Edit** button.

How it works...

The images that you uploaded to the product page will be displayed as thumbnails under **MORE VIEWS**, in the order that you specified. The labels that you entered will appear above each image. Shoppers can click the **Next >>** link to watch the visual story unfold.

Changing the layout of a product page

Magento enables you to customize almost every aspect of your store's appearance. However, this involves changing the layout templates, and is well beyond the scope of a book that focuses on quick solutions. You can, however, choose from a few different layouts for a product page. These layouts come with the standard Magento template.

How to do it...

1. Log in to your site's backend or Admin Panel.

2. Select **Catalog | Manage Products**. The **Manage Products** page displays. You will see a list of the products in your store.

3. For the product that you want, select the **Edit** link. The **Product Information** page displays. The **General** tab will be selected for you.

4. Select the **Design** tab.

5. From the **Page Layout** drop-down menu, select an alternate layout for the product page.

6. Save the product.

How it works...

The default Magento template contains several alternate layouts that you can use for your product pages. We will now show you each of those layouts, so that you can choose the one that best fits your product.

▶ The following screenshot shows the page layout with 1 column:

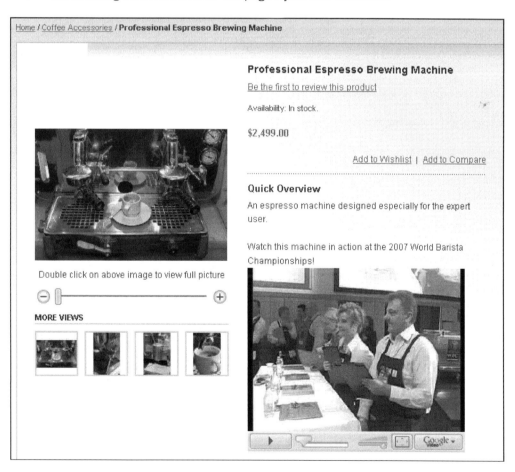

▶ The following screenshot shows the page layout with 2 columns with a left bar:

▸ The following screenshot shows the page layout with 2 columns with a right bar:

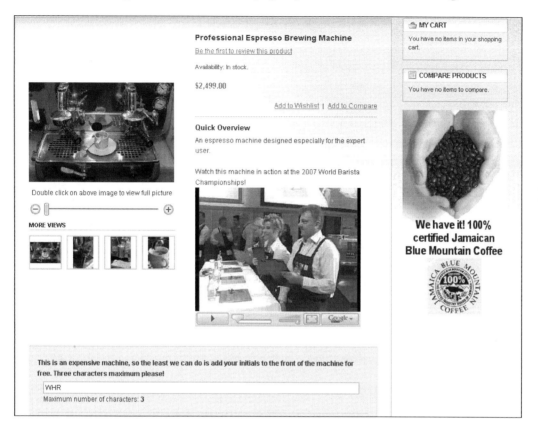

• The following screenshot shows the page layout with 3 columns:

Special pricing

Magento enables you to put products on sale. The sale price, or special price, is displayed with the normal price:

How to do it...

1. Log in to your site's backend or Admin Panel.

2. Select **Catalog | Manage Products**. The **Manage Products** page displays. You will see a list of the products in your store.

3. For the product for which you want special pricing, select the **Edit** link. The **Product Information** page displays. The **General** tab will be selected for you.

4. Select the **Prices** tab.

5. In the **Special Price** field, enter the special (or sale) price.

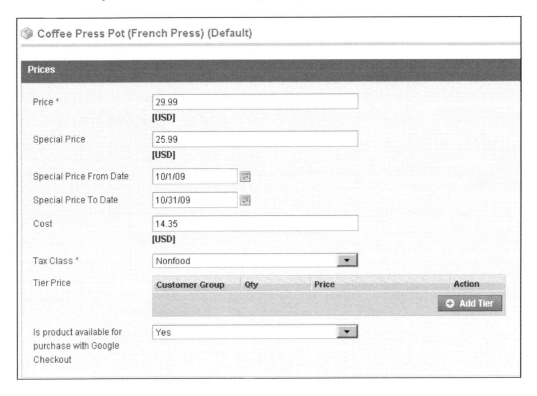

6. If you want the special price to be in effect during a specific date range, then enter the dates in the **From** and **To** fields. If you want the special price to be in effect until you remove it, then just leave the date fields blank.

7. Save and preview the product.

5
Increasing the Sale

Most store owners don't want their customers to buy products that the customers don't want. "Buyer's remorse" can lead to returned products and customers with bad feelings. However, we do want our customers to buy everything that they want. In other words, we want to maximize our sales using techniques that are both honest and effective.

Magento offers several techniques that we can use to maximize sales:

- ▶ Upselling with "You may also be interested in"
- ▶ Make additional sales with related products
- ▶ Make additional sales with custom options
- ▶ Offer cross-sells in the shopping cart
- ▶ Offer quantity discounts
- ▶ Offer free shipping

Each of these techniques is described below.

Upselling

In Magento, an upsell is a product that you would like your customer to buy, instead of the one that the customer is viewing. For example, suppose a customer is viewing a basic, hand-cranked coffee grinder; an upsell would be a more elaborate, expensive coffee grinder. Magento puts upsells at the bottom of a product page, under the heading **You may also be interested in the following product(s)**.

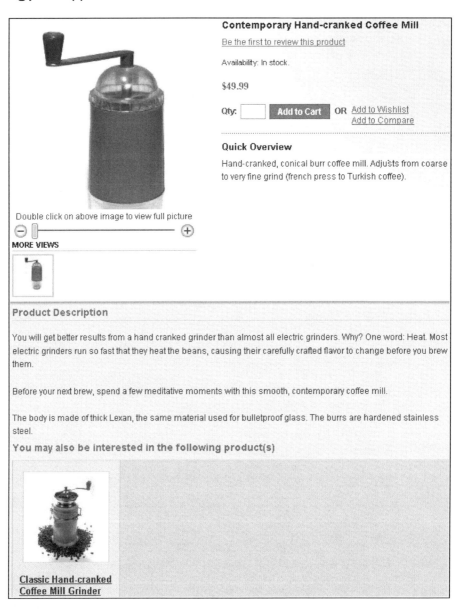

An upsell should yield a higher profit than the product the shopper is viewing. Matching an upsell to a product can be an art. The upsell needs to be more expensive than the current product, but not so expensive that the shopper immediately rejects the upsell. The upsell needs to offer clear advantages over the current product, without being so different that someone interested in the current product will consider it too different from what he/she wants. Also, the pictures and descriptive text for both products need to offer a direct and compelling comparison. All of these considerations are part of the art of upselling, which is beyond the scope of this cookbook. A web search on "the art of upselling" will produce many results. In this section, we will focus on the procedure needed to upsell in Magento.

Getting ready

Before you begin creating an upsell like the one pictured above, you should:

> ▶ Create the simple product for which you want an upsell. Ensure that it is in stock and enabled.

> ▶ Create the upsell product. Ensure that it is in stock and enabled.

How to do it...

1. Log in to your site's backend or Administrative Panel.

2. Select **Catalog | Manage Products**. The **Manage Products** page displays. You will see a list of the products in your store.

3. For the product that you want to upsell, select the **Edit** link. The **Product Information** page displays. The **General** tab will be selected for you.

4. Select the **Up-sells** tab. On this page, you will search for the upsell product.

5. Clear the check mark from the checkbox in the first column.

6. Enter the search criteria that will help to locate the upsell product. In this example, we know the product is not coffee, so it uses the **Default** attribute set instead of the **coffee-by-pound** attribute set.

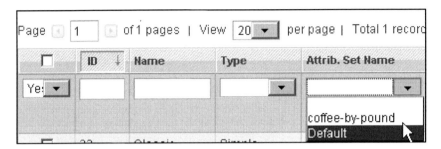

7. After entering or selecting the search criteria, click on the **Search** button.

8. For the product that you want to select, click to place a check mark in the checkbox:

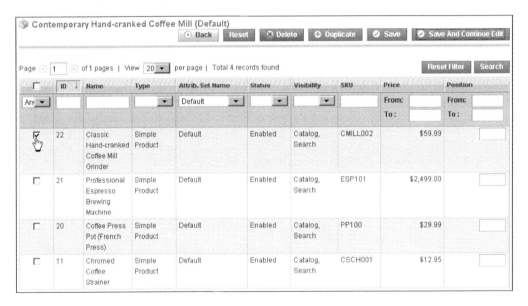

9. Click on the **Save And Continue Edit** button.

10. Preview the product to ensure that the upsell is displaying.

How it works...

In Magento's default template, upsells are displayed at the bottom of a product's page. If you want to move them to a more visible location, then you will need to edit the template for your product pages. You can find more information about editing templates in Packt's Magento template book.

Related products

In Magento, a related product is a product that you would like your customer to buy, in addition to the one that the customer is viewing. For example, suppose a customer is viewing a contemporary-styled coffee grinder. You might present the customer with a mug made in a similar, contemporary style.

Getting ready

Before you begin adding a related product like the one pictured above, you should:

▶ Create the simple product for which you want a related product. Ensure that it is in stock and enabled.

▶ Create the related product. Ensure that it is in stock and enabled.

How to do it...

1. Log in to your site's backend or Administrative Panel.

2. Select **Catalog | Manage Products**. The **Manage Products** page displays. You will see a list of the products in your store.

3. For the product that you want to add a related product, select the **Edit** link. The **Product Information** page displays. The **General** tab will be selected for you.

4. Select the **Related Products** tab. On this page, you will search for the related product.

5. Clear the check mark from the checkbox in the first column.

6. Enter the search criteria that will help to locate the upsell product. In this example, we know the product is not coffee, so it uses the **Default** attribute set instead of the **coffee-by-pound** attribute set.

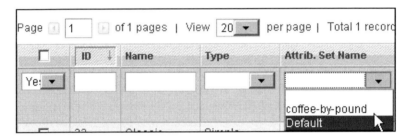

7. After entering or selecting the search criteria, click on the **Search** button.
8. For the product that you want to select, click to place a check mark in the checkbox:

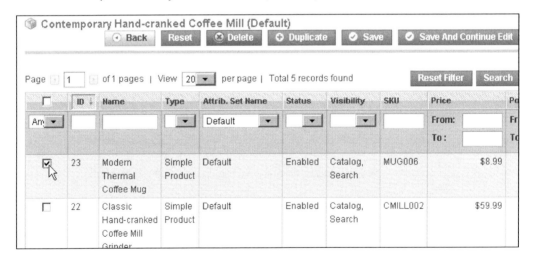

9. Click on the **Save And Continue Edit** button.
10. Preview the product to ensure that the related product is displaying.

How it works...

If you add a related product(s) to a product, Magento automatically displays the related product(s) in the **RELATED PRODUCTS** block. In Magento's default theme, the **RELATED PRODUCTS** block appears in the upper-right corner of the page. As long as you choose a layout that shows the right column, the block will appear automatically when you are viewing a product page and there is a related product to display.

Custom options

In Chapter 4, *Making the Sale by Optimizing Product Pages* we showed you how to use custom options to offer additional services and options for a product. As an example, we showed an espresso machine where the customer can add their initials to the machine. You can see that custom option immediately below the **MORE VIEWS** section:

In this example, the custom option was used to add value and expense to a product. You can also use the custom option to offer additional items. Our example here is a little different than the one in Chapter 4. We've added extra filter cups as another option. That is, we are using the custom option to offer accessories and spare parts for the main product.

Now let's compare this approach to related products, which is covered in the previous section. Related products are displayed in a separate block and that block always has the same title, **RELATED PRODUCTS**. Custom options are displayed in the same block as the main product. This shows the shopper that they clearly belong with the main product and you can customize the sales message. In this case, "**Extra filter cups are always a good idea!**"

The procedure for adding a custom option that is an accessory is the same as for adding a custom option that is a service or a customization.

How to do it...

1. Log in to your site's backend or Administrative Panel.

2. Select **Catalog | Manage Products**. The **Manage Products** page displays. You will see a list of the products in your store.

3. For the product that you want, select the **Edit** link. The **Product Information** page displays. The **General** tab will be selected for you.

4. Select the **Custom Options** tab.

5. Click the **Add New Option** button.

6. A new option appears. You will need to fill in the fields to complete this option.

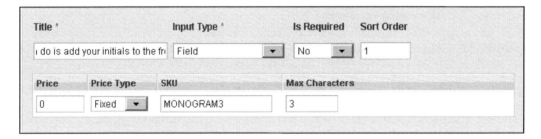

7. In the **Title** field, add text that will appear next to the option. The text that you see in the example above, "Extra filter cups...", was entered into the **Title** field. Consider making this title a sales pitch or call to action.

8. For the **Input type**, select one of the choices under **Select**. This is because the shopper will be selecting a product to add to the order. Based upon the type you select, other fields will appear. You will be required to fill in these other fields.

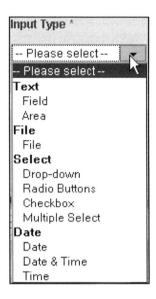

9. Add selections by clicking on the **Add New Row** button.

10. The **Is Required** drop-down menu determines if the customer must select this custom option to order the product. If you're just trying to offer accessories or spare parts, then you probably want to set this field to **No**.

11. The **Sort Order** field determines the order in which the custom options are displayed. They appear from the lowest to the highest.

12. The **Price** is a required field. If you set it to zero, then no price will display.

13. **Price Type** is **Fixed** if you always charge the same for that option. Setting it to **Percent** calculates the price for the option based on the price for the product.

14. **SKU** is not required, but if the option is another product (such as extra parts), then you will want to use it.

15. Save the product and preview it in your store.

Cross-sells

Have you stood at the checkout queue in a grocery store and noticed all the small, inexpensive merchandise that they place next to the register? Candy bars, tabloids, batteries, air fresheners for your car, the list goes on. Most people call these items "impulse purchases". They are small items that retailers tempt us with, as we wait for them to ring up our purchases.

Magento enables you to offer your online customers impulse purchases at checkout. We call these cross-sells. In the example below, the after-coffee mints are displayed as a cross-sell.

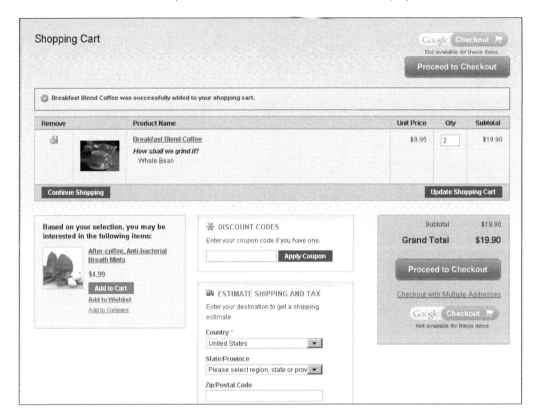

Unlike a physical store, the shopper is not held for a long time in the checkout queue. This means that online cross-sells need to be especially compelling for your customers to add them. However, online cross-sells do have an advantage that physical cross-sells lack. With Magento, we know what the shopper has in the shopping cart before he/she approaches the checkout. And so, during the checkout process, we can offer the shopper the kinds of cross-sells that complement the items the shopper has already chosen. In the preceding example, after-coffee breath mints make a good complement to the coffee in the shopping cart. If the shopper had bought a coffee press, then we might display a chromed coffee scoop as a cross-sell.

Just imagine if the impulse purchases next to the checkout queue changed, based upon the items that you have in your shopping cart.

Getting ready

Before you begin creating a cross-sell like the one pictured above, you should:

- ▶ Create the simple product for which you want a cross-sell. This doesn't work for configurable products. It only works for the simple products that make up a configurable product. Ensure that it is in stock and enabled.

- ▶ Create the cross-sell product. Ensure that it is in stock and enabled.

How to do it...

1. Log in to your site's backend or Administrative Panel.

2. Select **Catalog | Manage Products**. The **Manage Products** page displays. You will see a list of the products in your store.

3. For the product that you want to upsell, select the **Edit** link. The **Product Information** page displays. The **General** tab will be selected for you.

4. Select the **Cross-sells** tab. On this page, you will search for the cross-sell product.

5. Clear the check mark from the checkbox in the first column, and select **No** from the drop-down list below the checkbox.

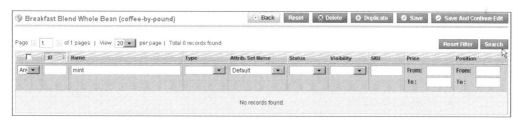

6. Enter the search criteria that will help to locate the cross-sell product. In the preceding example, we know the product is not coffee, so it uses the **Default** attribute set instead of the **coffee-by-pound** attribute set. And, it has the word **mint** in its **Name**.

7. After entering or selecting the search criteria, click on the **Search** button.

8. For the product that you want to select, click to place a check mark in the checkbox:

9. Click on the **Save and Continue Edit** button.

10. Switch to the frontend of your store. Add the product to your shopping cart, and ensure that the cross-sell is displaying.

Quantity discounts

In Magento, a discount given for buying more than one of a product is called **tiered pricing**. In the example below, you can see there are three price tiers:

Ethiopian Yrgacheffe Whole Bean

Be the first to review this product

Availability: In stock.

$14.00

‣ Buy 3 for **$11.90** each and *save 15%*
‣ Buy 6 for **$10.50** each and *save 25%*

Qty: [____] **Add to Cart** OR Add to Wishlist
Add to Compare

Quick Overview

Full bodied, citrusy, floral, with spicy sweet overtones. This wild grown coffee is the epitome of African coffee.

MORE VIEWS

The first tier is for buying 1 or 2 pounds at $14 per pound. The second tier is for buying 3 to 5 pounds at $11.90 per pound. The third tier is for buying 6 or more pounds at $10.50 per pound.

In our example store, the preceding tiers apply to any customer who visits the site without logging in. You can also create different pricing tiers for different groups of customers. This requires that the customer log in. Once the customer logs in, Magento (or you) can place that customer into a group. In our example store, we have pricing tiers for customers who have not logged in (anonymous visitors) and for customers who have created an account on our site and logged in:

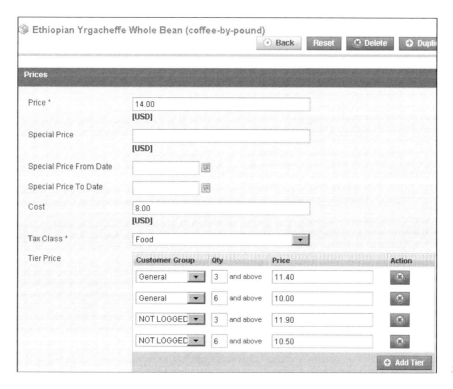

When a customer creates an account in our example store and logs in, he/she sees this on the product page. Note the welcome message for the logged-in customer in the upper-right corner of the page:

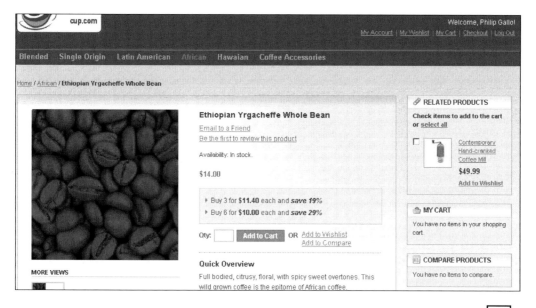

How to do it...

1. Log in to your site's backend or Administrative Panel.

2. Select **Catalog | Manage Products**. The **Manage Products** page displays. You will see a list of the products in your store.

3. For the product that you want to price, select the **Prices** tab.

4. Under **Tier Price**, there should be a blank row ready for you to fill out. If not, then click on the **Add Tier** button.

5. Under **Customer Group**, select the type of customer that will receive the tiered price.

This customer group...	Applies to...
ALL GROUPS	Everyone. This includes customers who have not logged in (anonymous visitors), and those who have.
NOT LOGGED IN	Customers who have not logged in. The customer might have an account on your site and be part of a group, but if he/she did not log in, then there's no way Magento would know that.
General	If you do not create a customer group and put the customer into that group, then the customer will, by default, belong to the **General** customer group.
...anything else...	The groups that you create under **Customers	Customer Groups** will appear in this drop-down list. You might create groups for business customers, non-profits, loyal customers, and more.

6. Under **Qty**, enter the minimum quantity the customer must buy to get this price.

7. Under **Price**, enter the price.

8. To add another tier, click on the **Add Tier** button.

9. Save and preview the product in your store. If you created different tiers for different customer groups, then remember to log in as a test customer and test the product.

Offering free shipping

To increase sales, you can offer free shipping for a minimum purchase amount. For example, "Free shipping on all orders over €100". This section shows how to offer free shipping on orders that meet a minimum amount. You can also offer free shipping on every order, but that is just a matter of entering zero for all shipping costs, so we will not cover it here.

 For the rest of this section, when we say "free shipping", we mean "free shipping for a minimum order amount".

If you always use the same shipping method, make free shipping an option under the shipper. This is the simplest option for you to set up. Free shipping becomes available only when the shopping cart reaches a minimum amount. In the following screenshot, you can see that the shopper has met the minimum amount of over $50:

Getting ready

Before you try to configure free shipping, you should know how to configure regular shipping, that is, you should have non-free shipping configured. This is covered in the *Magento Beginner's Guide*, and you can also find instructions online.

How to do it...

1. Log in to your site's backend, or Administrative Panel.
2. Select **System | Configuration**.
3. From the section listed on the left, select **Shipping Methods**.
4. In the upper-left of the page, from **Current Configuration Scope:**, select your website.

5. Scroll down to the shipper that you want to offer (**Table Rates**, **UPS**, **FedEx**, **USPS**, **DHL**).

6. As stated under the previous section *Getting ready*, this shipper should already be enabled and configured for non-free shipping.

7. Under **Free method**, select the method that you will offer for free shipping. For each order, you can offer only one kind of free shipping.

   In the following example, you can see that we offer **2nd Day Air** as the free shipping method. This means that if the customer's order meets the minimum requirement, the customer can choose (but is not required to choose), **2nd Day Air** free shipping.

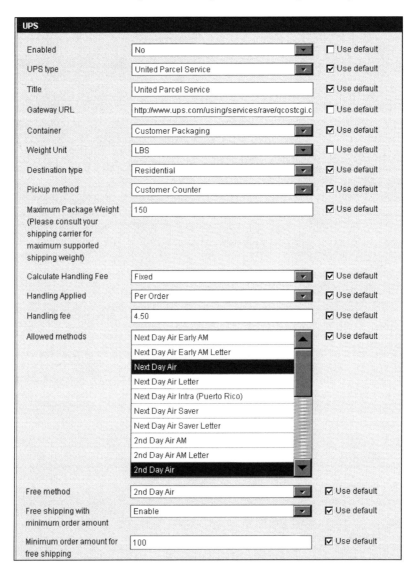

8. Under **Free shipping with minimum order amount**, select **Enable**.

9. Into the field **Minimum order amount for free shipping**, enter the minimum amount.

10. Save the configuration.

Advertising free shipping in the shopping cart side block

So now you offer free shipping for a minimum purchase amount. That's great. There's just one problem: Your customers don't know. They don't know because you haven't told them!

When you enable free shipping, your customer won't see it as a shipping option until he/she is checking out. So free shipping might come as a nice surprise to someone who has met the minimum purchase. But it won't encourage the customer to add more to their order unless you find a way to tell the customer.

One place where you can advertise free shipping is in the shopping cart side block that appears on every catalog page. In the following screenshot, you can see the side block labeled **MY CART**. Normally, this block displays only the number of items and the total. But we have added a message to the block: **We offer free shipping on orders over $100! Does your order qualify?**

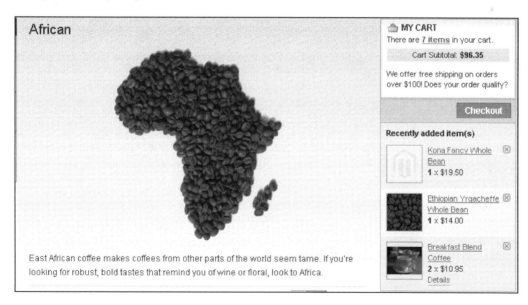

Now let's have a look at customizing the default theme. Your store's layout, terminology, color scheme, typestyles, and images are controlled by its theme. Creating an entirely new theme for your site is beyond the scope of this book. Covering that requires an entire book by itself such as *Magento Designer's Guide* from Packt.

Usually, when you customize your store's appearance, you want to create or install a new theme and customize that new theme. You leave the default Magento theme alone. However, as stated, creating or installing new themes is beyond the scope of this cookbook. Therefore, we will break the rules a little and customize a small part of the default theme.

 Be aware that when you upgrade Magento, it might install a new version of the default theme, and you might lose this customization. You might need to do this again.

Getting started

To perform this procedure, you must have access to Magento's files. You must be able to edit those files on the server.

How to do it...

1. Using an FTP client or HTML editor, locate this file:

   \app\design\frontend\default\coffee\template\checkout\cart\
   sidebar.phtml.

2. Open the file for editing. You can use DreamWeaver, WordPad, or any plain text editor.

3. In the file, find these lines. If possible, use your editor's find function to search for the words "Cart Subtotal:":

```
<div class="box base-mini mini-cart">
    <div class="head">
        <?php $_cartQty = $this->getSummaryCount() ?>
        <h4><?php echo $this->__('My Cart') ?></h4>
        <?php if ($_cartQty>0): ?>
            <?php if ($_cartQty==1): ?>
                <?php echo $this->__('There is <a href="%s">
                <strong>1 item</strong></a> in your cart.',
                $this->getUrl('checkout/cart')) ?>
            <?php else: ?>
                <?php echo $this->__('There are <a href="%s">
                <strong>%s items</strong></a> in your cart.',
                $this->getUrl('checkout/cart'), $_cartQty) ?>
            <?php endif ?>
            <p class="subtotal">
                <?php echo $this->__('Cart Subtotal:') ?>
                <strong><?php echo Mage::helper('checkout')-
```

```
>formatPrice($this->getSubtotal()) ?></strong>
<?php if ($_subtotalInclTax = $this-
>getSubtotalInclTax()): ?>
        <br /> (<strong><?php echo Mage::
        helper('checkout')->formatPrice
        ($_subtotalInclTax) ?></strong> <?php echo
        Mage::helper('tax')->getIncExcText
        (true) ?>)
        <?php endif; ?>
    </p>
  <?php endif ?>
</div>
```

4. Just before the last line, insert your sales message like this:

```
<?php endif ?>
<p>We offer free shipping on orders over $100! Does
your order qualify?</p>
</div>
```

5. Save the file.

6. Preview the results in your store.

6
Offering and Advertising Promotions

In this chapter, you will learn how to offer promotional pricing. Magento offers several ways of creating promotional pricing. The key difference between the various promotional pricing is when the discount is applied. For example:

- ▸ A Catalog Price Rule is applied when you view a product. The customer sees the discount as he/she browses the catalog.

- ▸ A Shopping Cart Price Rule is applied when a product is added to the shopping cart. The customer sees the discount after he/she adds the product to the shopping cart.

- ▸ A Coupon Code is applied during the payment part of checkout, after the customer enters a code into the shopping cart.

A **catalog price rule** is a change in price that is applied to a product before that product is added to the shopping cart. For example, we could offer "10 percent off on all coffee". Or, we could offer "20 percent off on all whole bean coffee". These are discounts that we want our shoppers to receive and know about before adding any items to the cart.

In the following screenshot, you can see the effect of a catalog price rule that gives a 10 percent discount on all coffee:

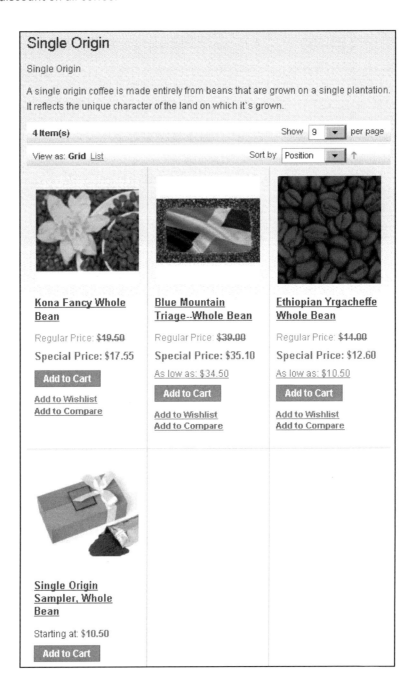

Notice that one of the products, the Single Origin Sampler, does not show the discount. That is because it is a grouped product. It consists of several simple products. The discount is applied to each of those simple products individually, like this:

A **shopping cart price rule** takes effect only after the shopper has added specific items to the shopping cart. For example, we could offer "10 percent off on all coffee purchases of $100 or more". Alternatively, we could offer a discount for buying specific items together. For example, "Buy this coffee grinder and French press together for a $10 discount". Clearly, the shopper must add items to the shopping cart before that rule takes effect.

In the following screenshot, we have applied that shopping cart rule. Notice the $10 discount is shown below the subtotal:

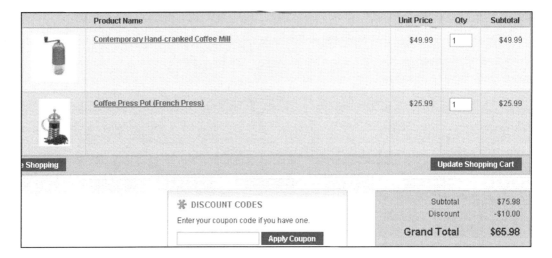

A **coupon code** is a special kind of shopping cart price rule. That is because a coupon is applied in the shopping cart. In the previous screenshot, you can see a place for the shopper to enter a coupon code.

Like any other shopping cart rule, a coupon can affect all or some of the items in the cart. Moreover, you can limit the number of times that a coupon is used.

Creating a catalog price rule

Remember that a catalog price rule will apply to all the products that meet its criteria. After you create and apply this rule, it will affect your entire catalog (at least, the parts of your catalog that meet its criteria).

Getting ready

You probably want your catalog price rule to apply to only specific products. In our example, we want the rule to apply to only coffee products. All of our coffee products use the attribute set **coffee-by-pound**. We will filter our products by that attribute set, so that the catalog price rule affects only coffee products.

Before you create a catalog price rule, you must decide which products you want the rule to affect. Then, you must determine what those products have in common. Do they all have the same attribute set? Do their SKUs begin with the same characters? Are they all in the same category or categories? Investigate and write down the criteria that you will use to filter the products for your catalog price rule.

How to do it...

1. Log in to your site's backend or Administrative Panel.

2. Select **Promotions | Catalog Price Rules**.

3. Click on the **Add New Rule** button. The **New Rule** page displays and the **Rule Information** tab is selected for you. You will enter basic information about the rule into this page:

4. Enter the **Rule Name**. Your customers will never see this. This is only so that the site administrator (you) can identify the rule in a list. Make it descriptive so you know what the rule does from the name.

5. Enter the **Description**. It is a good idea to put a plain language summary of the criteria and effect that the rule will have. Although it will not be seen by your shoppers, you might need this description as a reminder when you return to the rule.

6. Use the **Status** field to make a rule **Active** or **Inactive**. Later on, you will enter the effective dates for the rule. For the rule to take effect, it must be **Active** and have an effective date that is in effect now.

7. Select the **Customer Group**(s) to which this rule will apply. To select multiple groups, use *Ctrl*-click.

8. Enter the **From Date** and **To Date**. If you leave these blank, the rule will be in effect until you turn it OFF by making it **Inactive**. Unless you have a reason to leave these blank, enter from and to dates. Magento's behavior with blank date fields is sometimes erratic, and it is safest to specify the dates.

9. **Priority** determines how this rule will work with other catalog price rules. If several rules apply to the same product, then the one with the higher priority (lower number) will take effect first. Then, the next priority rule will take effect, and so on. This means that you need to keep track of all the catalog price rules that are in effect.

10. Select the **Conditions** tab.

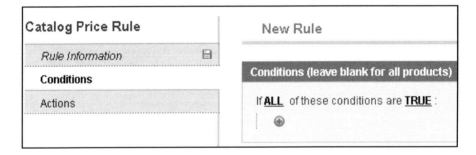

This is where you will enter the filter, which determines which products are affected by the rule.

 If you want the catalog rule to affect every single product in your catalog, then just leave this tab blank and move on to the **Actions** tab.

11. Do you want the rule to affect products that meet all of your criteria or any of your criteria? For example, if are putting only products made by the Wacky Widget Company on sale, then your condition would be:

ALL of these conditions are **TRUE**:

Manufacturer is Wacky Widget Company

But if you are putting products made by Wacky Widget Company and Worldwide Widgets on sale, then your condition would be:

ANY of these conditions are **TRUE**:

Manufacturer is Wacky Widget Company

Manufacturer is Worldwide Widgets

From the drop-down list, select **ALL** or **ANY**. Selecting **ALL** means that the rule will affect only those products where all of the conditions apply to the product. Selecting **ANY** means the rule will affect all products that match any of the conditions.

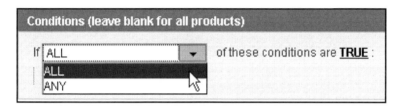

12. Select whether the conditions will be **TRUE** or **FALSE**.

13. If you want all of the products that have a characteristic, such as all the products that are over $100, then select **TRUE**.

14. If you want all of the products that do not have a characteristic, such as all of the products that are not coffee, then select **FALSE**.

15. Click on the green plus sign to add a condition:

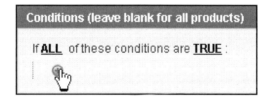

16. A drop-down menu appears where you will choose the type of condition to add:

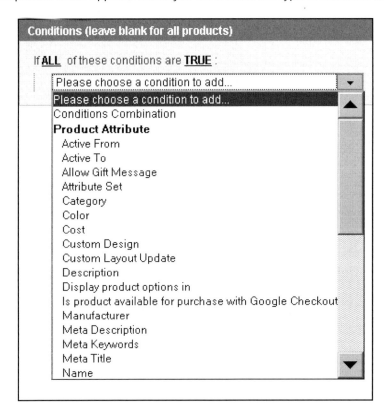

17. If you choose **Conditions Combination**, that will create a nested condition, like this:

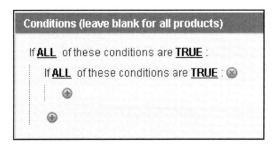

18. Nesting conditions like this can get complicated.

19. For this example, we will choose an attribute that we want to search for instead. Remember, we are searching for all of the products that are not coffee. In our store, we use the attribute set **coffee-by-pound** for all of our coffee products. So, we will select **Attribute Set** from the drop-down list:

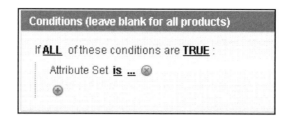

20. Select whether you want the attribute to match (**is**) or not match (**is not**) a specific value:

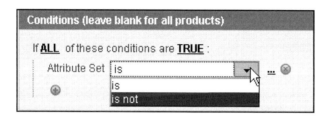

In our example, we are looking for all the products that are not coffee, so we will select **is not**.

21. Click on the dotted line:

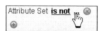

and then, from the drop-down list, select the value for the attribute:

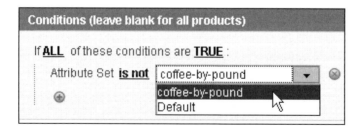

22. If you want to add another condition, then click on the green plus sign.

23. The result is a complete condition, which will apply this rule to only the products we want:

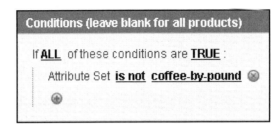

Let's choose the action now:

1. Select the **Actions** tab.

2. From the **Apply** drop-down menu, select the type of discount to apply:

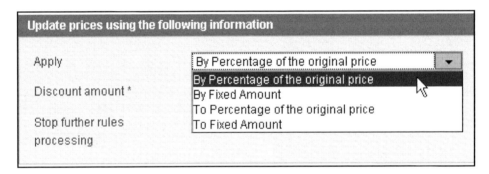

3. To offer a percentage discount, such as "15 percent off the original price", select **By percentage of the original price**.

4. To offer a dollar amount discount, such as "$10 off the original price", select **By Fixed Amount**.

5. To offer the product at a percentage of its original price, such as "70 percent of the original price", select **To Percentage of the original price**.

6. To offer the product for a fixed dollar amount, such as "All coffee for just $8.99 a pound", select **To Fixed Amount**.

7. In **Discount amount**, enter either the amount of the discount or the discounted price.

If you chose this for the Apply field...	Then enter this into the Discount amount field...
By Percentage of the original price	The percentage to subtract from the original price.
By Fixed Amount	The dollar amount to subtract from the original price.
To Percentage of the original price	The percentage of the original price that you will charge.
To Fixed Amount	The new sale price.

8. If you select **Yes** for **Stop further rules processing**, then no other catalog price rules will apply to these products.

9. Save the rule.

10. Return to the **Catalog Price Rules** page, and click on the **Apply Rules** button. If you don't do this, then your changes won't apply to your catalog.

How it works...

A catalog price rule is essentially a search condition that applies a discount. It searches your entire catalog of products (that is, your entire Magento website) for products that meet the conditions you specify and then applies the discount that you specify.

There's more...

A catalog price rule is especially useful for applying a discount to products that have something in common: the same category, the same attribute, the same manufacturer, and so on. But sometimes, you might want to discount a group of products that have nothing in common. For example, you might have products that are about to become obsolete, or they just aren't selling. In that case, you can create an attribute, like "deeply_discounted". Make the attribute a Yes/No choice. For the products that you want to put on sale, assign the value of Yes. Then create a catalog price rule that discounts products where deeply_discounted is Yes. Later in this chapter, we will look at how to create a clearance sale category.

Creating a shopping cart price rule and coupon

Remember that a shopping cart price rule will apply to all the products that meet its criteria, after those products are added to the shopping cart. The products that trigger the shopping cart price rule can be different from the products that are affected by it. For example, we will build a shopping cart price rule that applies a 10 percent discount to a coffee grinder, when it is ordered with a coffee press. The rule is triggered by the presence of the coffee grinder and the press in the cart together. It applies the discount to one of those products: the grinder.

Getting ready

Before you create a shopping cart price rule, you must decide which products you want to trigger the rule, and which products you want to affect. Then, you must determine how you will identify those products. Will you use the SKU? The name? The category? An attribute? Investigate and write down the criteria that you will use to filter the products that trigger the rule. Also write down the criteria that you will use to filter the products that are discounted by the rule.

How to do it...

1. Log in to your site's backend or Administrative Panel.

2. Select **Promotions | Shopping Cart Price Rules**.

3. Click on the **Add New Rule** button. The **New Rule** page displays and the **Rule Information** tab is selected for you. You will enter basic information about the rule into this page.

4. Enter the **Rule Name**. Your customers will never see this. This is only so that the site administrator (you) can identify the rule in a list. Make it descriptive so you know what the rule does from the name.

5. Enter the **Description**. It is a good idea to put a plain language summary of the criteria and effect that the rule will have.

6. Use the **Status** field to make the rule **Active** or **Inactive**. Later on, you will enter the effective dates for the rule. For the rule to take effect, it must be **Active** and have an effective date that is in effect now.

7. Select the **Customer Groups** to which this rule will apply. To select multiple groups, use *Ctrl*-click.

8. If you enter something into the **Coupon code** field, then this rule will take effect only if the shopper enters that same text into the **Coupon Code** field in the shopping cart. If you leave this blank, then no coupon code is needed to activate the rule.

9. If you enter something into the **Uses per coupon** field, then this rule can be activated only that number of times. You do not need a coupon to limit the number of times a shopping cart rule can be used. If you leave this blank, then it is unlimited.

10. If you enter something into the **Uses per customer** field, then this rule can be activated only that number of times per customer. You do not need a coupon to limit the number of times a shopping cart rule can be used by a customer. If you leave this blank, then it is unlimited. However, be aware that if you limit the number of uses per coupon, and do not limit the number of uses per customer, then one customer could theoretically use up the coupon.

11. Enter the **From Date** and **To Date**. If you leave these blank, then the rule will be in effect until you turn it off by making it **Inactive**.

12. **Priority** determines how this rule will work with other shopping cart price rules. If several rules apply to the same product, then the one with the higher priority (lower number) will take effect first. Then, the next priority rule will take effect, and so on. This means you need to keep track of all the shopping price rules that are in effect.

13. **Public in RSS Feed** determines if this rule will be published in your store's RSS feed. You can read more about using an RSS feed to keep in touch with your customers in chapter 7.

Let's go ahead and enter the conditions:

1. Select the **Conditions** tab.

   This is where you will enter the filter that determines which products are affected by the rule.

 If you want the shopping cart rule to take effect no matter which products are added to the cart, then just leave this tab blank, and move on to the **Actions** tab.

2. Do you want the rule to affect products that meet all of your criteria or any of your criteria? For example, we are offering 10 percent off a coffee grinder, if the customer also buys a coffee press. That means both the grinder and the press need to be in the cart. Our condition would be:

   ALL of these conditions are **TRUE**:

   An item is found in the cart with a SKU of CMHC001 (this is the grinder)

   An item is found in the cart with a SKU of PP100 (this is the press)

   From the drop-down list, select **ALL** or **ANY**. Selecting **ALL** means that the rule will take effect only if all the conditions are met. **ANY** means the rule will take effect if just one of the conditions is met.

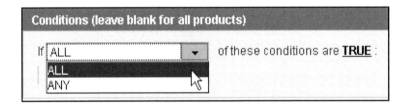

3. Select whether the conditions will be **TRUE** or **FALSE**. That is:

   If you want all of the products that have a characteristic, such as all the products that are over $100, then select **TRUE**.

   If you want all of the products that do not have a characteristic, such as all of the products that are not coffee, then select **FALSE**.

4. Click the green plus sign to add a condition:

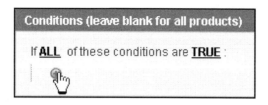

5. A drop-down menu appears, where you will choose the type of condition to add:

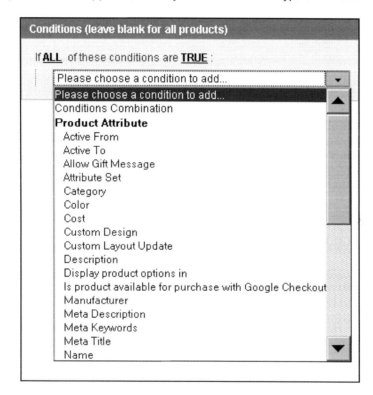

6. If you choose **Conditions Combination**, then that will create a nested condition, like this:

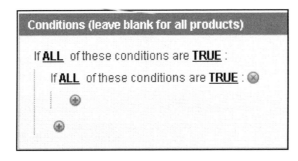

7. Nesting conditions, like this, can get complicated.

8. For this example, we will use the SKU to select the products that will trigger the rule. So, we will select **Product Attribute Combination** from the drop-down list. The result is a line like this:

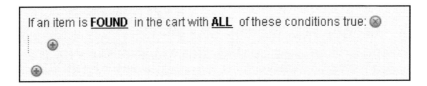

9. Choose **FOUND** or **NOT FOUND**. If you want the rule to be triggered when something is in the cart, then choose **FOUND**. If you want the rule to be triggered when something is not in the cart, then choose **NOT FOUND**.

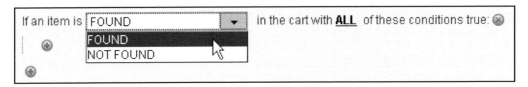

10. Select **ALL** or **ANY**. If you want the product to match every criteria that you enter, then select **ALL**. If you want the rule to trigger when a product matches at least one of the criteria, then select **ANY**.

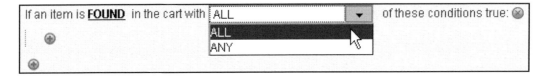

11. Click on the green plus sign to add a condition. In our example, we want to trigger the rule when two SKUs are found in the cart together:

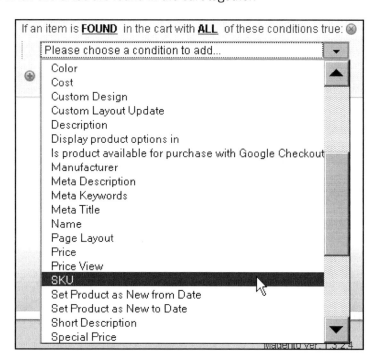

12. Select the comparison.

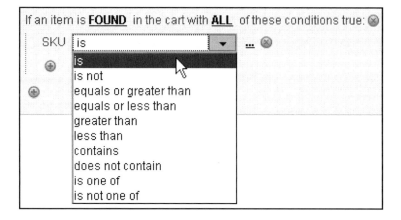

13. Click on the three dots to enter the value that you are comparing. In our example, we will enter the SKU of the coffee grinder.

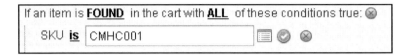

14. Now you have one complete condition. If you want to enter more conditions, then click on the green plus sign below the first condition. In our example, we have two conditions, and they both must be true for the rule to trigger:

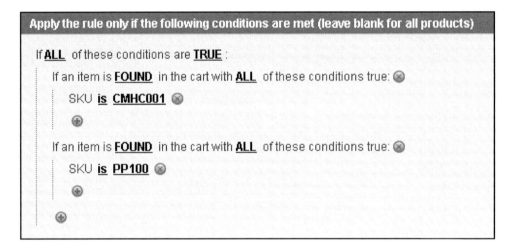

15. Select the **Actions** tab.

16. From the **Apply** drop-down menu, select the type of discount to apply.

17. To offer a percentage discount on just one product, such as "10 percent off a coffee grinder when ordered with a coffee press", then select **Percent of product price discount**.

18. To offer a dollar amount discount on just one product, such as "$10 off a coffee grinder when you purchase a coffee press", then select **Fixed amount discount**. This discount is deducted from the one product that you specify. So in this example, if the customer ordered two coffee grinders, then he/she would get $10 off each coffee grinder...for a total.

19. To offer a dollar amount discount on the entire shopping cart, such as "$10 off your order when you purchase a coffee grinder and coffee press together", select **Fixed amount discount for whole cart**. This discount is deducted from the cart. So in this example, if the customer ordered two coffee grinders, he/she would get $10 off the entire order...and only $10.

20. To offer a "buy this and get that free discount", select **Buy X get Y free (discount amount is Y)**. In this case, X can be one product, several products, or a combination of products.

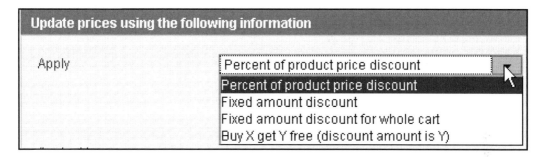

21. In **Discount amount**, enter either the amount or percentage of the discount.

22. In **Maximum Qty Discount is Applied to**, enter either the maximum number of products that the discount can affect. For example, if you offer "10 percent off the price of a coffee grinder with the purchase of a coffee press", and someone orders one coffee press and ten coffee grinders, then do you want to give them a discount on all ten coffee grinders?

23. If you selected **Fixed amount discount for whole cart**, then this setting has no effect.

24. In **Discount Qty Step(Buy X)**, enter the number of products that the customer must buy to receive the discount.

25. From the **Free shipping** drop-down menu, if you offer free shipping for the products affected by the rule, then choose whether just those products are shipped free or whether the entire order is shipped free.

26. If you select **Yes** for **Stop further rules processing**, then no other shopping cart price rules will apply to these products.

27. In the section **Apply the rule only to cart items matching the following conditions**, you can build a search condition that finds only the products to which you want to apply the rule. In our example, we want to apply the 10 percent discount to only one product, so we build a search condition that finds that product:

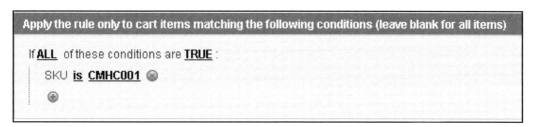

28. Save the rule.

29. Test the rule with your shopping cart.

Creating a clearance category

Creating a catalog or shopping cart price rule is a standard Magento technique. With a little extra effort, we can make these standard techniques even more effective. One way is to create a clearance category.

Getting started

Stores often have clearance sales, where they try to sell specific items at a deep discount. Sometimes, these items have nothing in common, except that the store owner wants to get rid of them. In a physical store, you might create a sale rack or clearance section. You would put all of these deeply discounted products into the clearance section.

You can also create a clearance section in your online store. Just like you created categories for different types of products (single origin coffees, blended coffees, African coffees, and so on), you can create a category for clearance products. And just as your other categories can appear in the site's navigation menu, the clearance category can appear in the navigation menu.

In a physical store, a product can appear in only one place in the store at a time. In your online store, a product can appear in multiple categories. This means that a clearance product can appear in both its normal categories and the clearance category. In our example store, the Ethiopian Yrgacheffe coffee appears in the categories **African** and **Clearance Items**:

How to do it...

1. Create a category for clearance items.

    ❑ Make it an anchor category. That is, it should be a child of the **Default Category**.

    ❑ You can use basic HTML to customize the description that appears on the category's landing page. Compare the HTML that you see in the screenshot below to the text that you see in the screenshot above. For more about this, see the *Add videos, links, and other HTML to product pages* section in Chapter 4.

    ❑ Choose an image for the clearance category that you think conveys the message, such as "This is the clearance rack!"

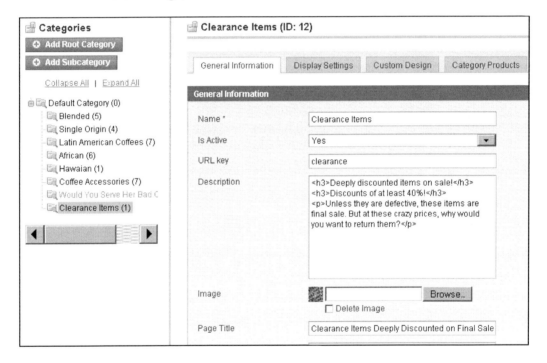

2. Add the product to the clearance category.

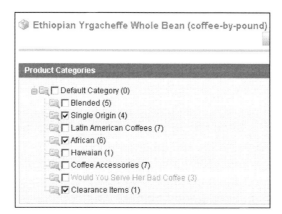

3. Check the product's pricing. Do you already have special pricing for this product? If so, then is that what you want? Remember, you're going to apply a discount to this product using a catalog price rule. Do you want to apply that catalog price rule in addition to a special price or instead of a special price?

4. Save the product.

5. Create a catalog price for the clearance category:

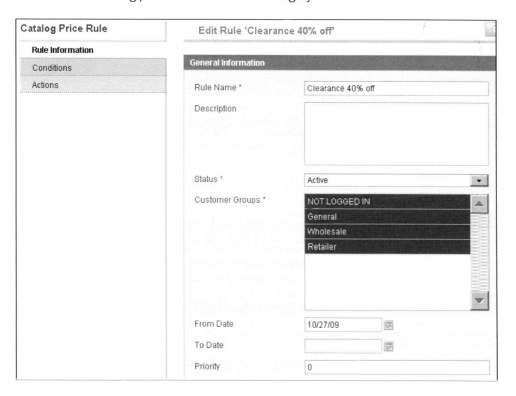

6. Create a condition that applies the catalog price rule to the products in the clearance category:

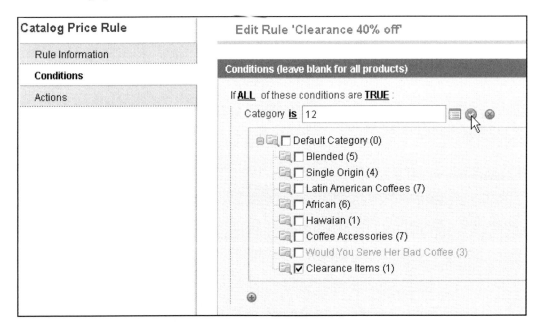

7. Specify the discount for the clearance category:

8. Save and apply the rule.

9. Preview the result in your store.

How it works...

In Magento, the `.phtml` files in `\app\design\frontend\default\template\` contain layout information for your site. By editing these files, you can change what information appears on your site, as well as where it appears. For more information on template files, refer to the "Designer's Guide to Magento" at `http://www.magentocommerce.com/design_guide`.

7
Engage Your Customers

In an online store, we do not have the opportunity to speak with our customers face-to-face. However, Magento offers several ways to engage your customers. Engaging your customers means giving them an opportunity to speak to you and others, and finding new ways to speak to them. That is the subject of this chapter.

In this chapter, you will learn how to engage your customers in a variety of ways:

- ▶ Produce and send a newsletter
- ▶ Let customers publish their wish list with an RSS feed
- ▶ Customize the customer's wishlist page with a message telling them to send their friends an RSS feed for their wishlist
- ▶ Determine which kind of social media is best for your business (Twitter, Posterous, Facebook)
- ▶ Add buttons to "Follow us on Twitter or Facebook"

Before using Magento's newsletter function, you must answer a very basic question: "How do customers sign up for my newsletter?" There are two ways:

- ▶ When a customer signs up for an account, they are given the chance to sign up for the newsletter.
- ▶ When a customer signs up for an account, they are automatically subscribed to your newsletter. The customer is not given the chance to opt out.

We will show you how to enable each of these options.

Cron job must be set up for newsletters to function correctly

A newsletter will never be sent if Magento's crontab is not set up. Several tasks (RSS, Newsletter, price alert, and more) are controlled by `cron.php`. Setting this up is part of the basic Magento installation. If you skipped this part of the installation, then you should go back and complete it.

Customizing transactional e-mails: Enable customers to opt into receiving newsletter

The newsletter module in Magento is enabled by default. However, if you don't see the newsletter options, then you might have disabled it by accident. Here is how to enable the module.

How to do it...

1. Log in to your site's backend or Administrative Panel.
2. Select **System | Configuration**.
3. From the left menu bar, select **Advanced**.
4. For **Mage_Newsletter**, select **Enable**.
5. Click on the **Save Config** button.

How it works...

When someone creates an account on your site, they will have the ability to opt into receiving the newsletter. Enabling the **Mage_Newsletter** setting creates the checkbox that you see in the following screenshot:

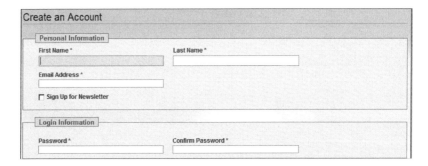

Enabling the newsletter also places the newsletter subscribe block on your site. By default, this block appears in the left column:

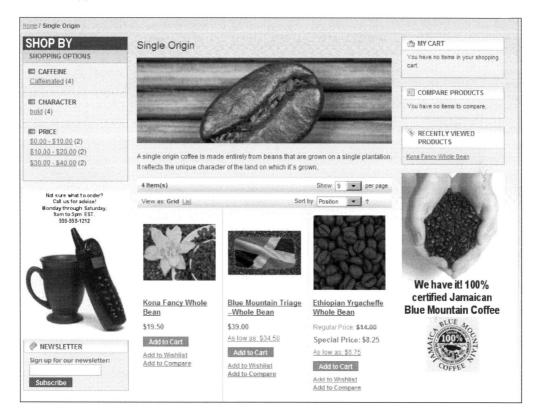

However, if you use a layout that doesn't show the left column, then you might want to move this block to the right column which is the subject of one of the procedures stated later in the chapter.

Automatically signing up customers for the newsletter

When the newsletter module is enabled, customers have the option to sign up for your newsletter. When the module is disabled, they cannot opt out of the newsletter. Instead, they are automatically added to the newsletter subscriber list.

How to do it...

1. Log in to your site's backend or Administrative Panel.

2. Select **System | Configuration**.

3. From the left menu bar, select **Advanced**.

4. For **Mage_Newsletter**, select **Disable**.

5. Click on the **Save Config** button.

How it works...

When someone creates an account on your site, they will automatically be added to your newsletter subscription list. They won't be informed about this, and they will not have the chance to opt out of receiving the newsletter. Before doing this, check the laws in your jurisdiction. Some places require you to inform your readers if you subscribe them to your newsletter. Disabling the **Mage_Newsletter** setting removes the checkbox that you saw in the previous screenshot:

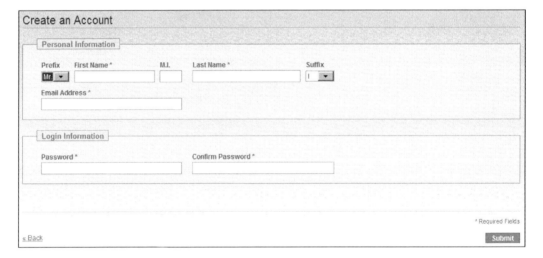

Moving the newsletter subscribe block to the right column

By default, Magento places the newsletter subscribe block in one of the columns. However, if you choose a layout that does not show that column, then you will lose the newsletter block. If that's the case, then consider moving it to the opposite column.

You will get a warning message: "You are about to customize the default theme". Your store's layout, terminology, color scheme, typestyles, and images are controlled by its theme. Creating an entirely new theme for your site is beyond the scope of this book. Covering that requires an entire book by itself, such as the *Magento Designer's Guide* from Packt.

Usually, when you customize your store's appearance, you want to create or install a new theme and customize that new theme. You leave the default Magento theme alone. However, as stated, creating or installing new themes is beyond the scope of this cookbook. Therefore, we will break the rules a little and customize a small part of the default theme.

[Be aware that when you upgrade Magento, it might install a new version of the default theme, and you might lose this customization. You might need to do this again.]

Getting started

To perform this procedure, you must have access to Magento's files. You must be able to edit those files on the server.

How to do it...

1. Using an FTP client or HTML editor, locate this file:

   `\app\design\frontend\default\default\layout\newsletter.xml`.

2. Open the file to edit it. You can use DreamWeaver, WordPad, or any plain text editor.

3. In the file, find these lines. If possible, use your editor's find function to search for the words "newsletter/subscribe":

   ```
   <!-- Mage_Newsletter -->
           <reference name="right">
               <block type="newsletter/subscribe"
        name="right.newsletter"

        template="newsletter/subscribe.phtml"/>
   ```

4. Change `reference name="right"` to `reference name="left"`.

5. Save the file.

6. Preview the results in your store.

Creating a newsletter

Now that you have enabled your customers to sign up for the newsletter, let's look at how you can create a newsletter.

How to do it...

Let's begin with creating templates:

1. Log in to your site's backend or Administrative Panel.

2. Select **Newsletter | Newsletter Templates**.

3. Click on the **Add New Template** button.

4. For **Template Name**, enter a name that will be meaningful to you. Your subscribers will never see this name, but you will see it in the list of templates.

5. For **Template Subject**, enter the subject line for the newsletter. When you send the newsletter via e-mail, this will become the subject line of the e-mail.

6. The **Sender Name** will be shown in your subscriber's e-mail as the name of the person who sent the newsletter.

7. The **Sender Email** will be shown in your subscriber's e-mail as the e-mail address of the person who sent the newsletter.

8. The **Template Content** is the content of your newsletter. This can be either plain text or HTML code.

Adding text to the newsletter:

1. Magento's newsletters are written in HTML, just like any other web page. However, Magento does not have an HTML editor. This means that you will need to produce your own HTML. You can either learn to write HTML by hand, or use a web page editor to write the newsletter and then copy the resulting HTML to Magento.

2. Obtain a basic HTML (web page) editor. It doesn't need to be fancy or have advanced features. Anything that enables you to easily produce HTML is fine. For some good, free HTML editors, check www.nonags.com.

3. Write and format the text of your newsletter. Do not put graphics into the newsletter yet.

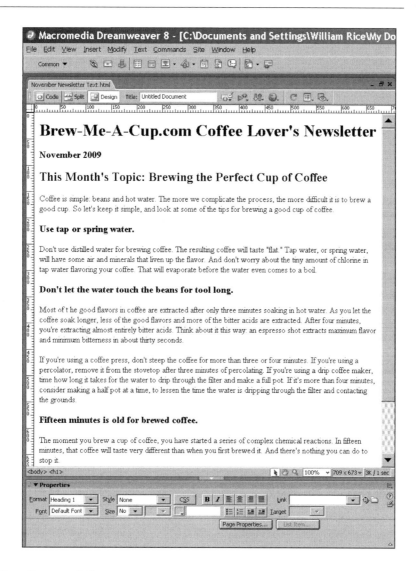

4. Save the newsletter.

5. Somewhere in your HTML editor, a menu function lets you see the HTML that it produced. It might be under the **View** menu or a **Mode** menu. For example, you might select **View | Code** or **View HTML**. Switch over to this HTML view mode.

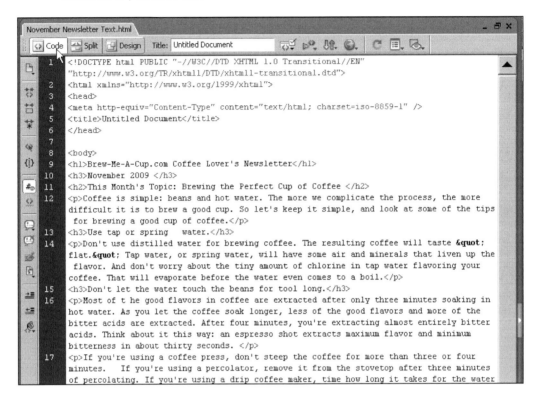

6. Select and copy all of the HTML code in between the `<body>` and `</body>` tags.

7. Switch to Magento.

8. Paste the HTML into the **Template Content** field.

9. Save the template.

Adding graphics to the newsletter:

1. Using your FTP client, upload the graphics for your newsletter to the `/media` directory on your web hosting server. If you want to organize the graphics, then create a subdirectory for this newsletter:

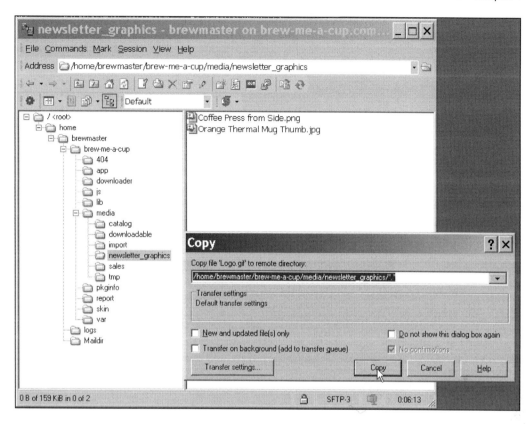

2. The URL for the graphics that we uploaded in the previous step will be:

`http://brew-me-a-cup.com/media/newsletter_graphics/filename`. So, to add a graphic to our newsletter, we will insert a link like this:

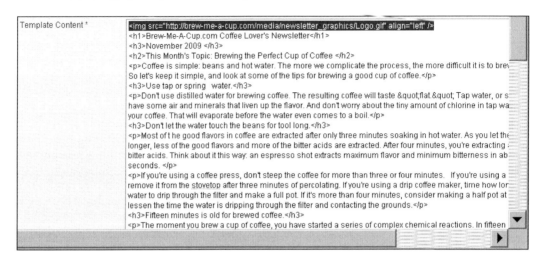

3. The result looks like this:

Now let's add links to the newsletter. The purpose of the newsletter is to drive traffic to your online store. Include links to help your readers get to your store.

1. Browse to the page that you want your readers to go to. For example, our newsletter mentions the french coffee press that we sell. So we would browse to that page in our online store.

2. Copy the URL (web address) of the product. In our case, it's `http://brew-me-a-cup.com/coffee-brewing-accessories/french-press-coffee-pot.html`.

3. Switch to Magento, where you are editing your newsletter.

4. Paste the link into Magento, as shown:

<h3>Fifteen minutes is old for brewed coffee.</h3>
<p>The moment you brew a cup of coffee, you have started a series of complex chemical reactions. In fifteen minutes, that coffee will taste very different than when you first brewed it. And there's nothing you can do to stop it.</p>
<img src="http://brew-me-a-cup.com/media/newsletter_graphics/Coffee Press from Side.png" align="left" /><p>Drink your coffee fresh. If you must hold it for a while, put it into a thermos or thermal carafe, where it will stay warm. Do not keep the coffee on the stovetop or on a hot plate. The heating element will continue to cook your brewed coffee, making it stale in only a few minutes instead of fifteen.</p>
<p>Better yet, brew the coffee fresh in front of your guests with our beautiful <href="http://brew-me-a-cup.com/coffee-brewing-accessories/french-press-coffee-pot.html">French Press.</a></p>

The result will look like this:

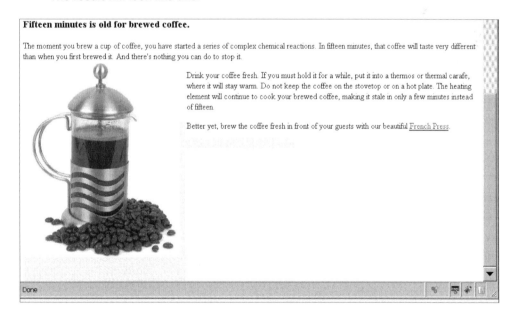

5. Save the template.

There's more...

You can add any HTML to a newsletter that you would to a web page. Just remember that Magento sends the text only. Therefore, if you want to include graphics, you must host those graphics somewhere and put links to them in the newsletter (as we did above). You can do the same with flash and media files.

Sending a newsletter

In this section, you start the process that will send out your newsletter.

How to do it...

1. Log in to your site's backend or Administrative Panel.

2. Select **Newsletter | Newsletter Templates**.

3. For the newsletter that you want to send, from the **Actions** drop-down menu on the right, select **Preview**.

4. The newsletter will open in a new browser window. You should always preview a newsletter before sending it.

5. Switch back to Magento.

6. If the preview looks good and you're sure you want to send the newsletter, then from the **Actions** drop-down menu on the right, select **Queue Newsletter....** The **Edit Newsletter** page displays.

7. Click on the calendar icon:

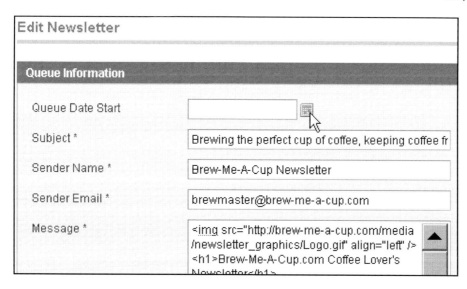

8. Click to select the date and time:

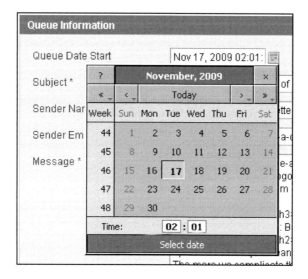

9. After selecting the date and time, close the pop-up window. You should see the date and time appear in the **Queue Date Start** field:

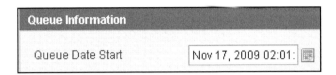

10. Click on the **Save Newsletter** button. Magento takes you to the **Newsletter Queue** page, where you will see the newsletter queued up and ready to send:

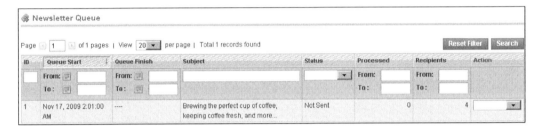

11. At the designated date and time, Magento will begin sending the newsletter. It will be sent in batches. Magento does this so that it does not overwhelm your Internet service provider.

Enabling customers to publish their wish list with an RSS feed

There are two parts to this process. First, you must enable customers to publish their wish list with an RSS feed. Then, you must encourage the customer to send the RSS feed to his/her friends.

However, the question then becomes, "Why would anyone subscribe to a customer's RSS feed for their wish list?"

A customer can share his/her wish list. In the following screenshot, notice the **Share Wishlist** button:

When a customer clicks this button, the customer is taken to a page where he/she can send a message to the person with whom he/she wants to share the wishlist:

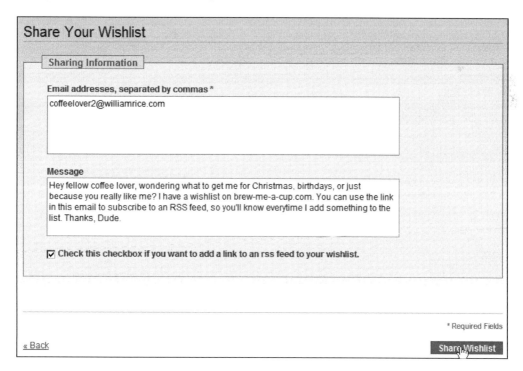

Notice the checkbox that adds an RSS link to the message. The first procedure below places that checkbox there.

Now we know why someone would subscribe to your customer's wishlist: because your customer sent them a message asking them to subscribe. However, another question you might want to answer is "How will your customers know that they can invite their friends to subscribe to their wishlists?" The short answer is: You must advertise wishlists and RSS feeds to your customers, and this is the subject of the second procedure below.

Getting started

In part two of this procedure, you must have access to Magento's files. You must be able to edit those files on the server. You can use any text editor, such as WordPad, or an HTML editor, like DreamWeaver.

How to do it...

In this section, we'll enable the RSS feed and customize the page where the customer signs up for the feed.

Let's begin by enabling the RSS feed for your customer's wishlist:

1. Select **System | Configuration | RSS Feeds**.

2. Under the **Rss Config** section, for **Enable RSS**, select **Enable**. You need to do this to enable any of the RSS feeds.

3. In the **Wishlist** section, for **Enable RSS**, select **Enable**. This will add an RSS link to your customer's wishlist page.

4. Save the configuration.

5. Now, when your customer uses the **Share Your Wishlist** page, he/she will see a checkbox to add the wishlist as an RSS feed to the message. Next, we need to inform and encourage your customer to use this feature.

6. Let's look at the customer's **My Wishlist** page again:

7. This would be an effective place to inform the customer that he/she can ask friends to subscribe to an RSS feed for the wishlist. To do that, we will need to edit the template for this page. This is part two of this process.

You will get a warning message: "You are about to create a new theme". Your store's layout, terminology, color scheme, typestyles, and images are controlled by its theme. Creating an entirely new theme for your site is beyond the scope of this book. Covering that requires an entire book by itself like the *Magento Designer's Guide* from Packt.

However, in this procedure, we will create a new theme with one file: the **My Wishlist** page. We will customize that one particular page. Magento will use the default theme for every other page in your store, except the one that we customize. This will give you some practice with themes and help you decide if you want to delve into customizing themes.

Now let's have a look at making a new theme and customizing the **My Wishlist** page with a message:

1. Assuming that you are using the default Magento theme, find the file `\app\design\frontend\default\default\template\wishlist\view.phtml`. You don't need to do anything with it yet. Just find it and make sure that you have access to it.

2. Create a new directory to hold the new theme. In our example, we called the new theme `coffee2`. So, we created this directory structure:

   `\app\design\frontend\default\coffee2\template\wishlist\`.

   Notice that we needed to create an entire directory structure, consisting of three new directories. Under `\app\design\frontend\default`, we created a new directory with our theme name, `coffee2`. Then, under `coffee2`, we created the directory `template`. Finally, under `template`, we created the directory `wishlist`.

3. Copy the file `view.phtml` from the directory you looked at in step 1 to the directory that you just created.

4. Open `vicw.phtml` in a text editor or an HTML editor.

5. Look for these lines. You might want to use your text editor's Search function to look for the word `endforeach`:

```
<?php endforeach ?>
</tbody>
</table>
<script type="text/javascript">decorateTable('wishlist-table')</
script>
<div class="button-set">
```

Between the lines `</table>` and `<script type=`, enter a new line. On this new line, add HTML code with the message that you want to give your customers. For example:

```
<?php endforeach ?>
</tbody>
</table>
<h3 align="center">Use the Share Wishlist button below to ask
friends to subscribe to your wishlist. When they subscribe, they
will be notified whenever you update your wishlist.</h3>
<script type="text/javascript">decorateTable('wishlist-table')</
script>
<div class="button-set">
```

6. Save the file.

7. Select **System | Configuration**. The configuration page displays.

8. From the **Current Configuration Scope** drop-down list in the upper-left corner of the page, select your store.

9. From the menu on the left, select **Design**.

10. Under the section for **Themes**, next to **Templates**, remove the check from the checkbox labeled **Use website**. Right now, your website is probably using the **default** theme.

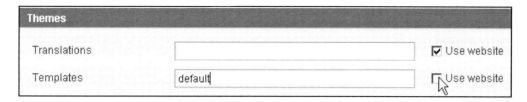

11. Erase the name of the template that is in the field, and enter the name of the template that you created.

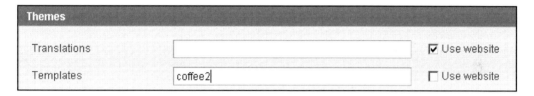

12. Save the configuration.

13. Preview the result in your store.

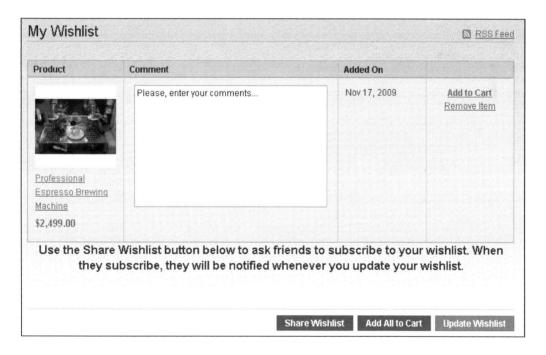

How it works...

At this point, you have a new template that consists of single file, the `view.phtml` that you just edited. In the next few steps, you will tell Magento to use this new template. This means that whenever Magento is displaying a page, it will check this template first for the layout, style, and content of the page. If Magento doesn't find the page in this layout, it will use the default layout instead. Since this template consists of only one file, for every page except this one, Magento will use the default layout.

Choosing the social networking site

Social networking sites can offer another way to connect with potential customers or another way to waste your time and get ignored. Choosing the right network and sending the right kind of content can help make your networking successful. By successful, we mean driving traffic to your Magento store.

In this section, we will briefly describe some of the more popular social networking sites. We will also look at how other businesses are using these sites to increase their profits.

When comparing social networks, the most important thing is not what features the network has, but how well its features fit into your store's and your customer's interactions.

Twitter

Twitter might be a good choice for keeping in touch with your customers if:

- You are highly mobile
- Your customers are highly mobile
- Your customers are interested in frequent, short updates from your business

Twitter messages, or tweets, are text-only. They are limited to 140 characters. This has several implications for how you would use Twitter to broadcast to your customers.

First, you need to be able to say something meaningful in 140 characters. For example, if you buy and sell comics online, you can send frequent updates on new stock: *Mike Grell's Green Arrow* issue #1 mint condition just arrived in stock.

`http://theworldscoolestcomicbookshop.com/greenarrow/grell-issue-1.`

Also, it helps if you and your customers have a shared vocabulary. Then you can use slang or abbreviations to compress ideas into fewer words. For example: Just acquired France 'Half Ecu' Coin Weight 010769 condition VF bids start at 30EU.

Those tweets illustrate another condition that helps make Twitter a successful tool for your business: quickly changing information. For our examples, we used a comic book shop and a coin shop, which have a constantly and quickly changing inventory. Another example of a quickly changing business that uses Twitter is lunch trucks. Many trucks use Twitter to inform their customers of their latest locations. For a live example, see `http://twitter.com/ TheTreatsTruck`.

Twitter enables you to easily send posts from your cell phone. If you have SMS (short message service) on your cell phone, you can update Twitter with it.

Twitter also enables your customers to easily follow your tweets, on their computer and also on their cell phones. If you do this, then you might want to point your customers to the Twitter help pages that tell how to receive your updates on their cell phones, at `http://help. twitter.com/forums/59008/entries/14014`. Alternatively, you can write your own directions and place them on a static page in your Magento site. (For directions on creating static pages, see the *Create a basic landing page* section in Chapter 3. These directions can be used to create a static web page with any content.)

Now, let's talk about what Twitter does not do as well as other services. First, at this time, you cannot send a picture via Twitter. You can get around this limitation by posting a picture to your Twitter account using a separate service like `www.twitpic.com`. This service is integrated with Twitter, so if you have a Twitter account, you have a Twitpic account. Twitpic enables you to upload a photo via your computer or cell phone. Then, a link to the photo is sent out on your Twitter account to your followers. You can include a message with the link. For example, here's a tweet from Grant Imahara, a co-host of the popular television series *Mythbusters*:

http://twitpic.com/pd1st - Now my robot army is complete! Thanks, @bunkbots!
8:53 AM Nov 13th from TwitPic

When one of his followers clicks the link, he/she is taken to the Twitpic site where the picture is hosted:

There are other Twitter photo sharing sites. These include:

- ▶ www.tweetphoto.com
- ▶ www.pikchur.com
- ▶ www.twitgoo.com
- ▶ www.yfrog.com
- ▶ www.piktor.com

Secondly, Twitter obviously can't be used to send articles, long messages, or multimedia. You can use it to send links to these things, but then you are sending your customer outside of the Twitter service.

Thirdly, interaction between you and your customers on Twitter is not as rich as it is on other social networks. You can send a tweet directly to a user, which Twitter calls a "direct message". But that message has the same character and format limitations as any other tweet, so it is no substitute for a long e-mail.

Fourthly, Twitter posts become stale and are forgotten very quickly. As new tweets appear on your customer's Twitter page, old tweets are pushed down the page and soon disappear. If the information that you share with your customers is something they would want to refer to tomorrow, then Twitter is not your best choice. But, if the information goes stale quickly, and you want an immediate response from the customer, Twitter can be a good choice.

If your customers will want frequent, short updates about your store, they or you are highly mobile, you only occasionally need to send them pictures or longer messages, and you want to keep only the freshest information in front of your customers, then Twitter can be an effective way to communicate with them. Just remember that you must advertise that you're Twittering or your customers will never know that they should be following you.

This section focused on how you can use Twitter to reach out to your customers. You can also enable your customers with Twitter accounts to send tweets about your store's products to their friends. In a later section, we will see how to place a "Tweet this" button in your site's footer. In the meantime, here are directions on how you can place a "Follow us on Twitter" button in your Magento store.

How to do it...

Let's place a **Follow Us on Twitter** button in the Magento footer. To put a Twitter button on your site, you will go to the Twitter site to get the HTML code needed. Then, you will add that code to your site.

Let's begin by getting the Twitter button code:

1. Log in to your Twitter account.
2. From the bottom of the Twitter page, select the link for **Goodies**.
3. On the **Twitter Goodies** page, select the link for **Buttons**.
4. At the bottom of the **Buttons** page, you can choose between "Follow Us on Twitter" or "Follow Me on Twitter". Choose the one that's most appropriate for your business.
5. Select the button that you want to use. A pop-up window appears with HTML code that you need to copy.
6. Copy the code. You might want to paste it into a blank document or even an e-mail to save it for when you need it.

Now, to paste the Twitter code into the Magento footer:

1. Log in to your site's backend.
2. Select **CMS | Static Blocks**.
3. Select **Footer Links**. An editing page for the links in your store's footer is displayed. By default, the footer includes links for **About Us** and **Customer Service**.
4. Paste the Twitter button code into the footer. Like the other links, place it between the tag `<li>` and `</li>`:

```
<ul>
<li><a href="http://www.twitter.com/brewmeacup"><img src="http://
twitter-badges.s3.amazonaws.com/follow_us-b.png" alt="Follow
brewmeacup on Twitter"/></a></li>
<li><a href="{{store url=""}}about-magento-demo-store">About Us</
a></li>
<li class="last"><a href="{{store url=""}}customer-
service">Customer Service</a></li>
</ul>
```

5. Click on the **Save Block** button.

6. Preview the result in your frontend. You should see the **Follow Me on Twitter** button in the footer of your store.

There's more...

The links in Magento's footer are easy to customize because they are in a static block that you can edit directly from the backend. Most social networks enable you to copy and paste code for buttons like the Twitter button that we previously added. Before you copy the code, make sure that you are logged into the social network under your store's account and not your personal account. This is because the code that you copy contains a pointer to the account that is logged in at the time that you copy the code.

Also, check the Magento official site for a Twitter extension. Because this extension is not part of the core Magento code, you should check to ensure it works with the version of Magento that you are using. Adding this extension might be easier than modifying your layout.

Posterous

Like Twitter, Posterous makes it easy for you to post from a mobile device. Using a smartphone (such as an iphone, Blackberry, or Android phone), you can post text, pictures, and video from anywhere. Of course, you can also post from your computer.

But "there is no free lunch", so there is a tradeoff for being able to post rich media from your phone. Posterous cannot send your posts to a cell phone as short messages. Customers who follow you on Posterous can be notified of new posts by text message or e-mail, but the entire post will not be sent, only a notification that there is a new post. Your customers will need to read your posts on their computers.

If pictures, audio, or video are important to your marketing and you need to post while away from your desk, then Posterous can provide a good solution. Moreover, if you want to be able to post from your e-mail client instead of needing to log in to another web page, then right now Posterous provides the easiest solution.

Consider this scenario:

You are an antiques dealer. You spend a lot of time away from your office searching for antiques to buy and resell. One Saturday, while at an estate sale, you purchase a Queen Anne desk to resell in your shop. You take some photos of the desk with your Blackberry and add a sales message: "*Just acquired this beautiful Queen Anne desk at an estate sale! Original finish, tiger stripe mahogany, solid silver hardware. On Monday morning, check the front page of our site for details and price*". Early Monday, you add the product to your Magento site and feature it on the front page.

Your customers have had all weekend to look over the new piece on your Posterous blog. And when they log in to their regular e-mail on Monday, they'll see your notice to check the front page of your Magento site for the new piece.

Posterous' biggest advantage is its ability to post to multiple sites all at once. You can configure your Posterous blog so that posts are automatically reposted to other services: Twitter, Facebook, Flickr, WordPress, Tumblr, Blogger, Typepad, Movable Type, Livejournal, and Xanga.

 If your customers are likely to be found on several social networks, then Posterous can be the hub from which you send postings to all those networks at once.

If, after reading this section, you decide that you need to keep your customers constantly informed with Twitter and also educated with longer blog pieces, then consider using Posterous to accomplish both from the same place.

Here's another advantage: Easy posting for your customers. Sending posts to your Posterous blog is as easy as sending an e-mail. It can also be that easy for your customers. Posterous can make it especially easy for you to run a contest where your customers enter a photo, video, audio clip, bookmark, slogan, and so on. Customers can just e-mail their entries to post@yourblogname.posterous.com.

Consider using Posterous for these kinds of contests:

- ▶ Send in a photo of yourself using a specific product. The winning photo gets a store credit.
- ▶ Send in a cell phone video clip of a product in use. The winning video appears on the product page and gets a refund for the amount of the product.
- ▶ Send in a slogan for a new category of products. The winner gets a product from that category.

Let's use Posterous to run a customer photo contest.

How to do it...

1. Go to www.posterous.com and sign up for a Posterous account. Make your Posterous page name something like yourstorename.posterous.com.

2. On the **Manage** page for your Posterous account, under the **Settings** tab for the drop-down menu labeled **Who should be allowed to post on your site?**, select **Anyone can post, I will moderate**. Save the setting.

3. Announce your contest on your Magento site. You will probably use a static page, or even the front page, of your site for this:

4. As posts are e-mailed to your Posterous blog, log in to Posterous, select the **Manage** page, and then the **Posts** tab:

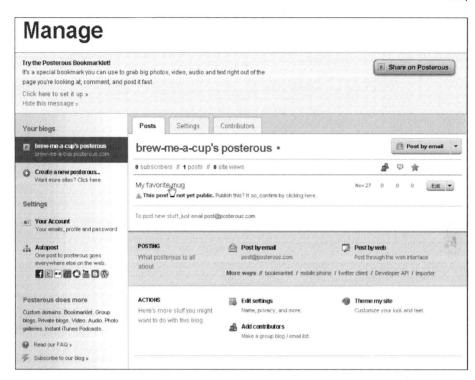

5. As shown, click the title of the post to preview it. This will show the post as your readers will see it if you approve it:

6. Go back to the **Manage** page. Next to the post, select the **Edit** drop-down menu:

7. If the post is inappropriate, then **Delete** it. If you plan to post it, then you should probably **Tag** it with the name of your contest. This enables you and your readers to find the contest posts.

8. Click the link labeled **clicking here** to make the post public. It will be added to your blog.

Let's make your Posterous blog ready for business.

How to do it...

You might have heard the saying, "It's nothing personal, it's just business". You should keep this in mind when working on any social networking site. Remember that the goal of any social networking is to drive business to your online store. So, treat your Posterous page like it's part of your business image. Populate it with information that leads back to your store. Select a name and theme that reflect your store's identity.

1. Make sure the site name and site subhead accurately convey your business and help to guide people back to your online store:

2. While logged in to Posterous, from the front page of your blog, click on the link for your profile. Posterous will notify you that you haven't entered any profile information. Click the link to enter profile information and save it.

3. On the **Manage** page, under **Settings**, select the button to **Theme and Customize My Site**. Then select a theme that most closely matches (or complements) your business.

4. Under **Posting and Commenting**, choose whether to allow readers to comment or not.

5. From the left bar, select **Your Account**. This brings you to the **Your Contact Info** page. On this page, enter the e-mail address(es) from which you want to be able to post. You can also enable posting from your mobile phone.

6. Select the tab for **Your Profile**. Fill out the bio and upload a picture that is appropriate for your store (for example, you store's logo).

Facebook

Twitter is an excellent tool for broadcasting short messages to your customers. And Posterous makes it very easy for your customers to send you feedback, contest entries, reviews, or any other postings that you've asked them for. However, neither of them is as good at community building as Facebook and its rivals (MySpace, Xanga, LiveJournal, and others).

Respond to customers

Here is an example of a retailer's Facebook page. Notice the second comment in the conversation, where a customer states he could not find a product in his size. Three comments later, an employee of the store offers to try to find it for the customer:

If your customers will feed off of interacting with each other and with your staff, then a feature-rich community site like Facebook might be a good choice for you. Consider Facebook if enthusiasm for your product or service is improved by customer interaction.

Remember, the interaction will be mostly unfiltered. It will also be immediate. For example, a book shop might post book reviews on its Facebook page. If the shop allows customers to comment on the books, then they should be prepared for the occasional unfiltered, off-topic, or even offensive comment. The shop can delete these after they're posted, but it cannot prevent them.

The most important Facebook tip

If you have a Facebook page for your online store, then you need to monitor it so that two things do not go unattended: postings that could damage your business, and customer questions.

Creating events

On our coffee store's page, you can see that we posted an event to our Facebook page:

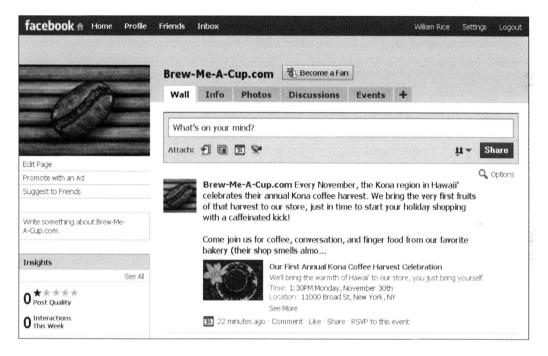

Other Facebook members can RSVP (reply) to the event announcement. They can also share the event, and if you've allowed, invite others.

There are some things that Facebook events do well:

▶ Facebook makes it easy for fans of your page to spread news about your event.

▶ If you take replies (enable RSVP), then you can see who is invited, who responded, and even print a guest list for the event.

▶ Facebook gives you and the attendees a place to upload photos and write comments about the event.

And, there are some things that Facebook events do not do so well:

- ► You cannot limit the number of people who attend an event. If the number gets too large, then you could "become a victim of your own success".

- ► You cannot tell who invited whom. You don't know if your event "went viral" because one dedicated customer invited a lot of friends or if the effort was more dispersed.

How to do it...

Obviously, you can use Facebook events to plan events for your existing customers. But the real benefit of using Facebook is its networking abilities. You want your event to "go viral". This means that you want your customers, who are Facebook fans of your page, to spread word of your event. Facebook enables you to add a personal message to the invitation e-mail that you send to your Facebook friends and fans. Use this personal message to encourage them to invite their friends.

Also, periodically mention the event on your Facebook page. On Facebook, new content appears at the top and old content is pushed down. Periodically mention the event, preferably in a way that is a little different each time, to keep it near the top of the page.

After the event, you can use Facebook to follow up and thank the people who attended.

In all cases, remember that the business purpose of a Facebook event is to spread the word about your Magento store. Make the event something that people will want to share with their friends.

Post photos and videos

You can use this to share photos or videos that might not be appropriate for your online catalog, but that help to build interest in your products. For example, if you sell ski equipment, then you could post videos of the most impressive sections of nearby ski runs. And of course, in the description for the video, you would link back to the pair of skis or snowboard that would be perfect for this ski run. A fan of howies posted this video of Ugandan children learning to say the store's name:

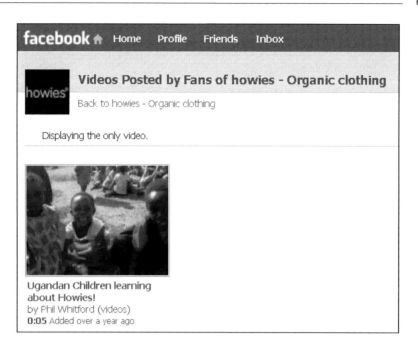

Facebook enables you to post photos and videos on a page that you own, and it also enables your customers to upload their own photos and videos. You can use this for:

- ▶ Customer contests. Photos showing your product in the most unusual place, or videos showing the most outrageous use of your product. For example, a bicycle shop might have a contest for the most impressive photo of someone airborne, using at least one of their products. Link to this contest announcement directly from your Magento store.

- ▶ Customer education. Create a photo album with step-by-step photos and brief captions that show how to do something fun or unique with your product. For example, a store that sells hairstyle products might create a photo album showing how to create an outrageous hairstyle with one of their products. Link this album directly to the product page in Magento and also link to from the product page.

- ▶ Community building. Post photos and videos of store events. For example, if a jeweller actually travels to where the gemstones are mined to purchase them, he/she might post pictures and videos of the trip. Link the Facebook album directly to the products in the Magento store that use these gems, and mention the exotic source of the gems in the product descriptions.

In each case, remember that the business purpose of posting photos and videos on Facebook is to generate sales. So whenever possible, try to link each video, album, or even photo, back to a specific product or category in your Magento store.

Discussions

On Facebook, you and your customers can engage in discussions:

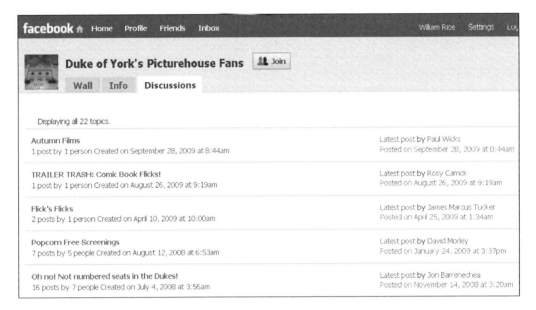

Like most Facebook features, discussions are open to anyone. You do not have the option of approving or rejecting comments before they are made. Be aware of this before you allow discussions on your Facebook page.

How to do it...

Facebook discussions can be a good way to present ideas to your customers and get their feedback. For example, in the previous screenshot, the topic **Popcorn Free Screenings** was started when someone asked about the idea of having a food-free movie night a week.

If you do this, then try to link to the Facebook discussions page from your Magento store. For example, suppose our coffee store uses a discussion to find out what kinds of coffee our customers want us to stock:

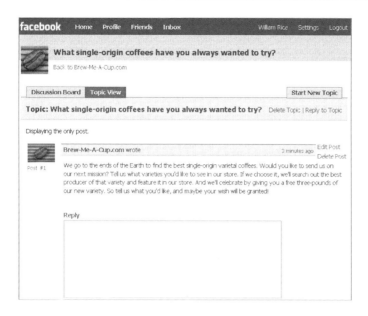

In our Magento store, on the category page for single origin coffees, we modified the description to include text and links about this discussion:

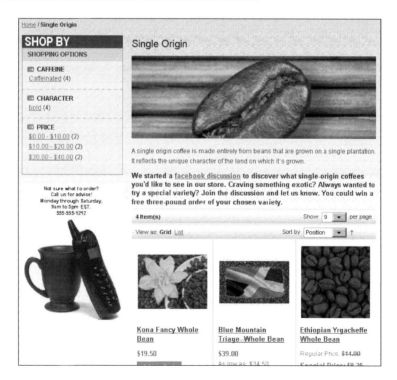

In addition to starting discussions yourself, you should also pay special attention to discussion topics that are started by your customers. These unsolicited discussions can reveal things about your business that make your customers passionate, pleased, and displeased.

The second-most important Facebook tip

Many business owners get caught up in using Facebook to expand their customer base. Remember that on Facebook, or any social network site, it is your current customers who will spread the news about your business. Pay special attention to their discussions. Even if they are not writing directly to you, they are telling you something. And if you want them to do your marketing for you, then you need to listen and respond to them.

Sign up for a Facebook page

Let's learn how to sign up for a Facebook page.

How to do it...

A Facebook page is a public profile for your business. It is like a personal Facebook page because it gives you many of the same tools as when you sign up for a personal account. However, there is a difference:

Facebook pages are for businesses. Facebook profiles are for personal use. It is against Facebook's terms of service to use a personal profile for profit. If you are a business, you must set up a page and not a profile. Facebook has been known to terminate personal profiles that were created not for people, but for businesses.

To set up a Facebook page for your business, follow Facebook's excellent instructions at `http://www.facebook.com/advertising/?pages`.

Customizing transactional e-mails

There are many events which trigger an e-mail from Magento to your customer:

▶ When the customer places an order, Magento sends a confirmation e-mail.

▶ When someone creates an account on your site, Magento sends a welcome e-mail.

▶ When you update an order in Magento with shipping information, Magento sends the customer a shipping update, and many more.

All of these e-mails must be customized for your store! In the default Magento installation, these e-mails use "Magento Demo Store" as the name of the store. They use (800) DEMO-STORE as the phone number of the store. And, they include e-mail addresses that point to the makers of Magento. If you don't customize these e-mails, then you will be sending confusing and possibly embarrassing messages to your customers.

There are two ways to customize these e-mails. One way is to edit the template files that are supplied with Magento. You can find directions on how to do this on the Web. However, if you just edit the standard templates that came with Magento, when you upgrade Magento, these standard templates will be replaced with new standard templates. And those new standard templates will have the "Magento Demo Store" information in them again. You will lose your customizations.

The other way takes longer, but is the correct and safer way to customize Magento's e-mail templates. We will cover that method here.

How to do it...

1. In the Admin interface, select **System | Transactional Emails**.

2. Select the **Add New Template** button. The **New Email Template** page displays:

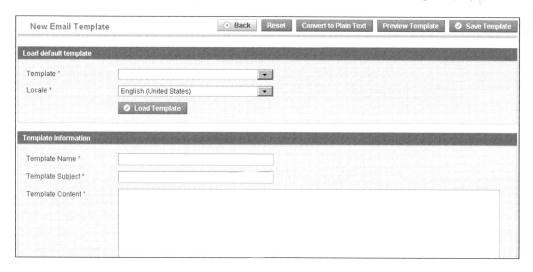

3. From the **Template** drop-down list, select the first e-mail template available. In the default installation, this is **New admin password**.

4. From the **Locale** drop-down list, select the language that you are using for your store.

5. Select the **Load Template** button.

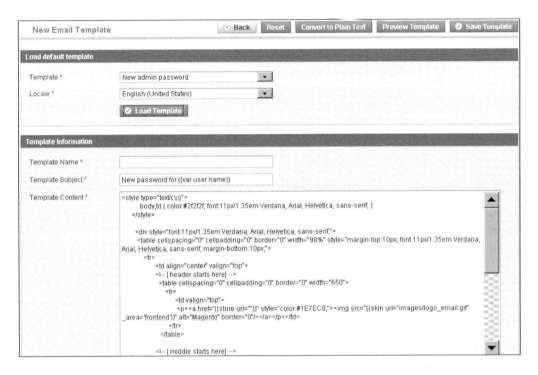

This is the default template, which contains the "Magento Demo Store" information. You will save this template under a different name and customize it with your store's information.

1. In **Template Name**, enter a prefix of your own, followed by the default name of the template. For example, **Customize: New admin password**.

2. The **Template Content** is the body of the e-mail. This is what your customer receives. You must replace the default, fictional information in the body with your store's information. The easiest way to do this is to copy the code out of the **Template Content**, paste it into a word processor, use find and replace to replace the fictional information, and then copy-and-paste it back into Magento.

3. Click inside the **Template Content**.

4. From your browser's **Edit** menu, select **Select All**.

5. From your browser's **Edit** menu, select **Copy**.

6. Launch your favorite word processor such as WordPad or Text Editor.

7. In a blank document, paste the code that you copied out of the **Template Content**.

8. Use your word processor's find and replace function to:

Find this text...	...and replace it with this text...
`alt="Magento"`	`alt="Your Store's Name"`
	(where `Your Store's Name` really is the name of your store).
`Magento Demo Store`	The name of your store.
`mailto:magento@varien.com`	`mailto:your store's email address`
	(where `your store's email address` really is the e-mail address of your store).
`dummyemail@ magentocommerce.com`	`mailto:your store's email address`
	(where `your store's email address` really is the e-mail address of your store).
`(800) DEMO-STORE`	The phone number of your store.
`Monday - Friday, 8am - 5pm PST`	Your store's customer service hours.

9. Once again, use **Edit | Select All** to select all of the text in the word processor.

10. Switch over to Magento.

11. Delete the existing template content.

12. Paste the text that you edited.

13. Save the template.

14. Preview the template. If needed, make more changes and save again.

 Repeat this for each e-mail template in the **Template** drop-down list.

In the default Magento installation, there are 36 e-mail templates. Customizing them all will probably take two or three hours. This is tedious, but it is necessary. And if you do it using the previous method instead of editing the template files directly, your changes will still be there after you upgrade Magento.

There's more...

If your word processor can record and play back macros, then consider making one that will perform the "find and replaces" in the preceding table. It will take a few extra minutes to record the macro. But once you do, you will be able to edit an e-mail template in seconds instead of minutes.

Also, as you preview each e-mail template, consider if you want to change more than just the store information. Does the default text convey the style and attitude that you want for your store? Does it help to build rapport with the customer and strengthen your store's image? Even a simple confirmation e-mail is a chance to express your store's brand and make the customer feel good.

8

Let Your Customers Speak

Magento has tools that enable you to communicate with your customers. In Chapter 6, we looked at tools that you could use to speak to your customers. In this chapter, you will learn about some tools that enable your customers to speak with you and others:

- ▶ Reviews
- ▶ Ratings
- ▶ Polls
- ▶ Tags
- ▶ E-mail to a friend

Customer reviews

In Magento, you can give your customers the ability to review a product. Other shoppers can see the review and also post their own reviews. By default, Magento requires all reviews to be approved by the store administrator. Reviews do not appear until you review and approve them.

Now let's have a look at reviews from the customer's point of view. When a shopper views a product that has not been reviewed, he/she sees a link on the product page inviting the customer to review the product:

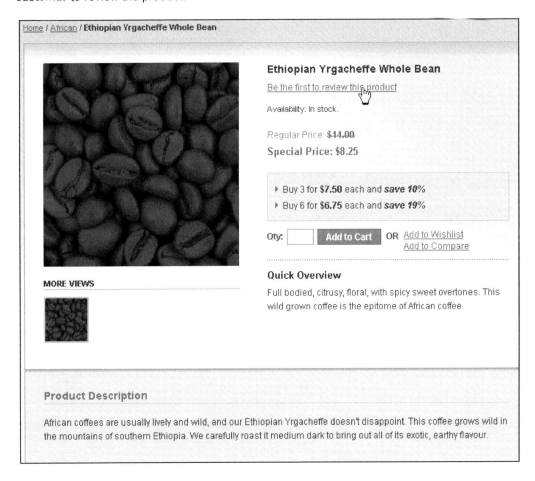

The customer is then taken to the review form:

Ethiopian Yrgacheffe Whole Bean

Be the first to review this product

Availability: In stock.

Regular Price: ~~$14.00~~

Special Price: $8.25

‣ Buy 3 for **$7.50** each and *save 10%*
‣ Buy 6 for **$6.75** each and *save 19%*

Qty: [ ] **Add to Cart** OR Add to Wishlist
Add to Compare

« Back to Main Product Info

Write Your Own Review

You're reviewing: Ethiopian Yrgacheffe Whole Bean

Nickname*

CoffeeHead

Summary of Your Review*

The best gourmet-to-dollar ratio I've ever tasted!

Review*

This African coffee is every bit as complex, fruity, and smooth as the more expensive Blue Mountain and Kona. Brew it quickly: no more than three minutes in a French press or under a drip maker. Then add a little more hot water to get the concentration you want. You will be amazed.

After the customer submits the review, Magento displays a confirmation message at the top of the page. Notice that the review must be approved before it is posted:

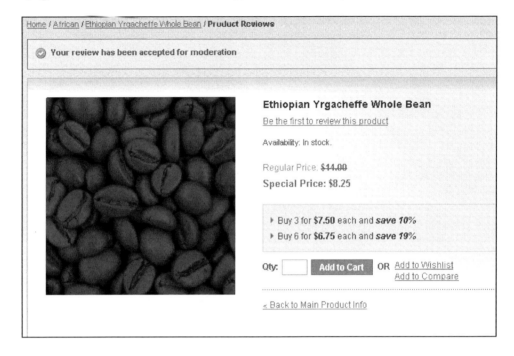

This is where you, the site administrator, enter the process. You will review, edit, and approve or deny the review. Instructions for each of those tasks appear next.

Enabling reviews

If you do not see the **Review** link beneath a product's title, then this indicates that the Review module is not enabled.

How to do it...

1. From the administrative interface, select **System | Configuration**.
2. In the upper-left corner, from the drop-down list, select your store.
3. From the left menu, under the **ADVANCED** sub menu, select the **Advanced** option.
4. In the main window area, for **Mage_Review**, select **Enable**.
5. Save the configuration.

Moderating reviews

Moderating reviews means approving or denying the reviews submitted by your readers.

How to do it...

1. From the administrative interface, select **Catalog | Reviews and Ratings | Customer Reviews | Pending Reviews**. This displays the reviews that need moderation, as shown in the following screenshot:

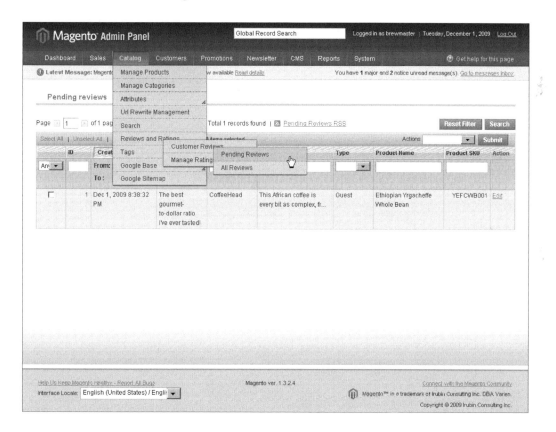

2. For the pending review, select the **Edit** link. This displays the editing window for the review:

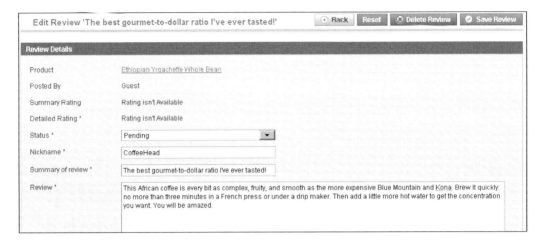

3. In the **Edit Review** page, you can edit any part of the review.

4. To approve or reject the review, select from the **Status** drop-down list:

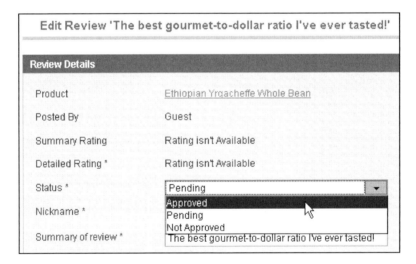

5. After you approve the review, a link to the review appears on the product page:

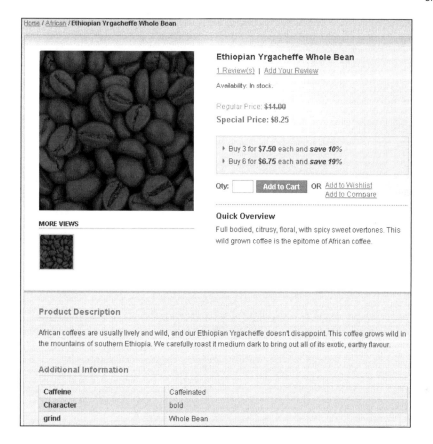

How it works...

The Reviews module is enabled by default in Magento. If it's not enabled on your site, then you can use the directions we mentioned to enable it. Ultimately, you are in complete control of all reviews submitted by your customers. You can approve, deny, and change their reviews at will.

There's more...

You should set a store policy about editing reviews. Will you always post reviews exactly as the customer wrote them, or will you correct spelling or grammar mistakes? Will you shorten reviews if they contain information that is not helpful? Will you allow negative reviews? Will you respond to reviews by inserting comments into them? You need a policy to deal with these questions, and consider posting that policy on a static page or the **Customer Service** page.

Because you can enter reviews from the backend, you can use something other than Magento to collect reviews. For example, you could hold a contest on Facebook where people vote on the best review. Facebook's "Like this" feature can be used to collect the vote. Whoever gets the most "Like this" votes, wins the contest.

Customer ratings

In Magento, you can give your customers the ability to rate a product on a scale of one to five stars. You can offer one or more criteria for the rating. As with reviews, you must approve each rating before it appears in your store.

In the following example, you can see that the **Ethiopian Yrgacheffe Whole Bean** coffee received a five-star review:

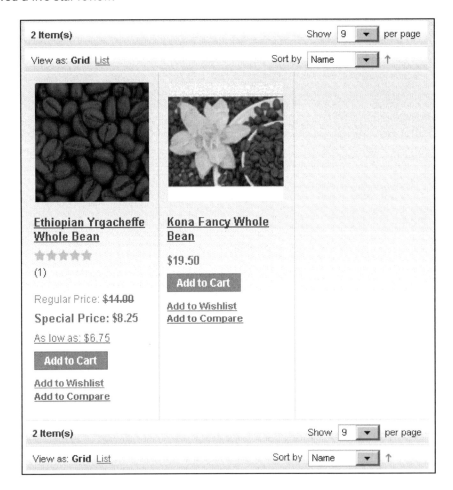

For a customer to see the ratings, he/she must go to the product page, and then click the **Reviews** link. This displays the **Reviews** page for that product:

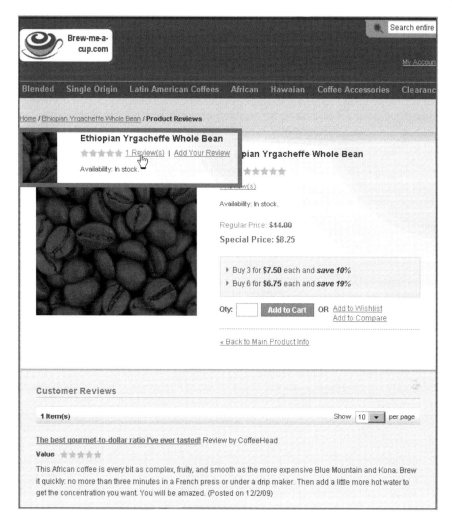

Enable ratings

First, you must enable the ratings module so that readers can submit ratings for a product.

How to do it...

1. From the administrative interface, select **System | Configuration**.

2. In the upper-left corner, from the drop-down list, select your store.

3. From the left menu, under **ADVANCED**, select **Advanced**.

4. In the main window area, for **Mage_Rating**, select **Enable**.

5. Save the configuration.

Apply one of Magento's default rating scales

In this procedure, you will determine which qualities a customer can rate.

How to do it...

1. Select **Catalog | Reviews and Ratings | Manage Ratings**.

2. Click on the rating scale that you want to enable. The default scales are **Quality**, **Price**, and **Value**.

3. If you have different stores, each will be listed on this page. If you want the rating scale to have a special name in a store, then enter it next to the store name.

4. Under **Rating Visibility**, select the store(s) in which you want the rating to appear. If you don't do this, the rating will not appear in your store(s).

5. Click on the **Save Rating** button.

Create a rating scale

In this procedure, you will determine the name of the rating scale that your customer sees.

How to do it...

1. Select **Catalog | Reviews and Ratings | Manage Ratings**.

2. Select the **Add New Rating** button. The **New Rating** page appears.

3. For **Default Value**, enter a name for this rating scale. This will be the name that you will see in the administrative interface, as well as the one your customers will see.

4. If you have different stores, each will be listed on this page. If you want the rating scale to have a special name in a store, then enter it next to the store name.

5. Under **Rating Visibility**, select the store(s) in which you want the rating to appear. If you don't do this, the rating will not appear in your store(s).

6. Click on the **Save Rating** button.

How it works...

Using ratings involves three steps: enabling the Ratings module, choosing the product qualities that are rated, and creating a scale for the rating. As with reviews, you must approve all ratings before they are applied to a product.

Polls

In Magento, a Poll is a single question with some multiple-choice answers. You can ask any question you want. Your shoppers get to select only one of the answers:

After voting, the shopper sees the result of the poll till date:

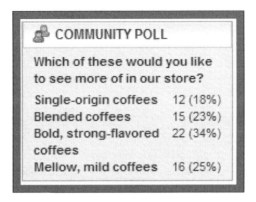

What can you do with a poll?

Your poll can be serious or silly, informative or entertaining. Here are some ideas:

Have some fun

Make your polls fun, so that they become one of the reasons people visit your site. A good example of this is the polls on `http://slashdot.org`. This is a site for technology, with the motto "News for nerds. Stuff that matters". Another good example is `http://thinkgeek.com`, which has a survey page. This is a site that sells gadgets that appeal to technology fans. Almost any one of the questions on their survey page would make a good poll question. Let's take a look at a few of these sites and discuss what makes their polls or surveys so attractive to their audience. First, a few polls from `www.slashdot.org`:

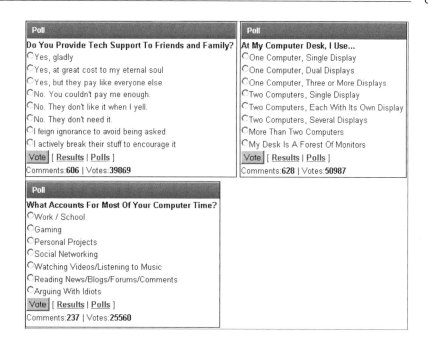

And, the survey page from www.thinkgeek.com:

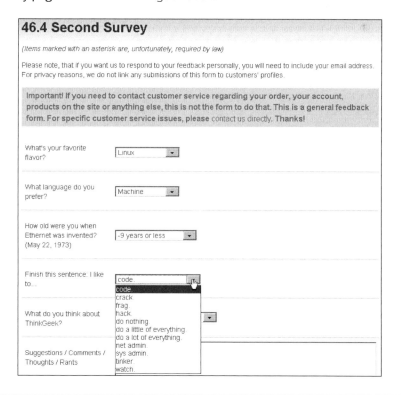

First, notice that the questions are specific to the topic of the site. The first Slashdot poll asks about providing tech support to family. This is a constant topic of conversation (and complaint) among technology workers. In the ThinkGeek survey, one of the questions even gives the reader some interesting trivia. Both of these questions draw upon the culture of the site's audience. They are almost "inside jokes" among the readers and shoppers to whom they are targeted.

Second, notice that the questions are about the reader, not the site or the store. They ask what the reader likes, or what the reader does. In short, they ask for the kind of information that people like to share about themselves when they're having conversations.

And third, notice that at least some of the answers are clever, sarcastic, or even a little outrageous. Some of the answers are exactly the kind of witty thing that you wish you had said when someone last asked you this question.

Among the kind of people who visit your store, is there a topic that is guaranteed to start an intense conversation or stimulate jokes? For example, if you sell movies, you might ask visitors to vote on the best movie lines ever. Or focus even more tightly on your audience. One Irish movie rental store, `www.screenclick.com`, ran a poll on the "Worst Irish Accent in a Movie" (the winner: Tom Cruise in *Far and Away*).

Do the visitors to your site have a common experience that they discuss often? For example, if your site sells imports from Germany, you might ask them to choose their favorite German beer.

Make at least one answer funny or witty. Give the visitor to your site a chance to feel clever by choosing that answer.

Or, be sincere

Polls can also be a way to connect to your customers and find out what they want. More importantly, you can use a poll to find out what your customers want from you.

In our first example, we showed a poll question asking customers what kinds of coffee they wanted to see more of in our coffee store. You can also ask visitors about the shipping options you offer, how your store is organized, and the type of product information they want to see.

If you ask your customers what kind of improvements they want to see in your store, then be prepared to actually make those improvements. And when you introduce the improvement, you can announce it on the front page, or in a static block, as something that your customers asked for.

Remember, anyone can answer

Remember that any visitor to your store can answer a poll question. They don't need to purchase anything or even create an account on your site. As you interpret the results of a poll, keep in mind that you are seeing the opinion of visitors to your store, not just customers.

If you want to conduct a survey of just your paying customers, then your newsletter subscribers are the best list you will find in Magento.

How to do it...

Let's go ahead and create a poll:

1. Select **CMS | Poll Manager**.

2. Select the **Add New Poll** button. The **New Poll** page appears.

3. In the field **Poll Question**, enter the text of your question. This is the question that your customers will see.

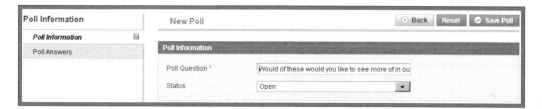

4. For **Status**, select **Open**. This makes the poll visible in your store.

5. Select the **Poll Answers** tab.

6. Click on the **Add New Answer** button. Fields for **Answer Title** and **Votes Count** are displayed:

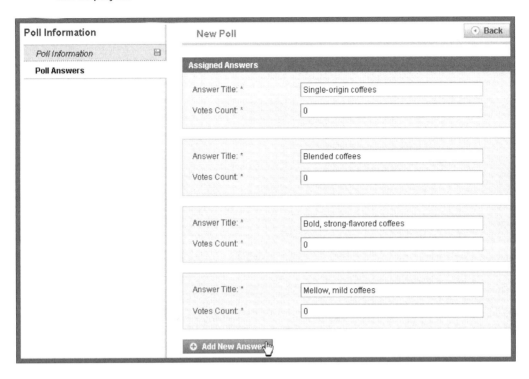

7. In the field **Answer Title**, enter the text of the answer. This is the answer that your customers will see.

8. In the field **Votes Count**, enter the starting number of votes. As people select this answer, they will add to this starting number.

9. Save the poll.

Tagging

Tags are descriptive words that your customers, or you, assign to a product. A tag is usually a single word. While customers can add tags to a product, the store administrator must always approve the tags.

Customers add tags to a product and see the tags assigned to a product at the bottom of the product's page:

Ethiopian Yrgacheffe Whole Bean

Email to a Friend

★★★★★ 1 Review(s) | Add Your Review

Availability: In stock.

Regular Price: $~~14.00~~

Special Price: $8.25

▸ Buy 3 for **$7.50** each and *save 10%*

▸ Buy 6 for **$6.75** each and *save 19%*

Qty: [   ] **Add to Cart** OR Add to Wishlist
                                      Add to Compare

MORE VIEWS

Quick Overview

Full bodied, citrusy, floral, with spicy sweet overtones. This wild grown coffee is the epitome of African coffee.

Product Description

African coffees are usually lively and wild, and our Ethiopian Yrgacheffe doesn't disappoint. This coffee grows wild in the mountains of southern Ethiopia. We carefully roast it medium dark to bring out all of its exotic, earthy flavour.

Additional Information

Caffeine	Caffeinated
Character	bold
grind	Whole Bean
Roast	Full City (medium dark)

Product Tags

Add Your Tags:

[exotic bold smooth value]   **Add Tags**

Customer tags do not appear immediately on the product page. They must be approved by the store administrator. The customer will receive a message that the tags have been accepted for moderation:

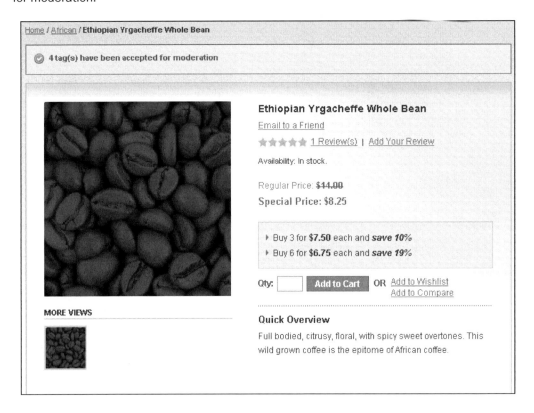

Later in the chapter, we will cover how to approve and reject tags.

When the first product in your store has been tagged, a tag cloud will appear. This tag cloud gives shoppers another way of finding products that interest them:

How to do it...

Let's have a look at enabling or disabling tagging:

1. From the administrative interface, select **System | Configuration**.

2. In the upper-left corner, from the drop-down list, select your store.

3. From the left menu, under **ADVANCED**, select **Advanced**.

4. In the main window area, for **Mage_Tag**, select **Enable** or **Disable**.

5. Save the configuration.

How to do it...

Now let's moderate (Approve or Reject) tags submitted by customers:

1. From the administrative interface, select **Catalog | Tags | Pending Tags**. The **Pending Tags** page appears. It lists all of the tags that you need to either approve or reject:

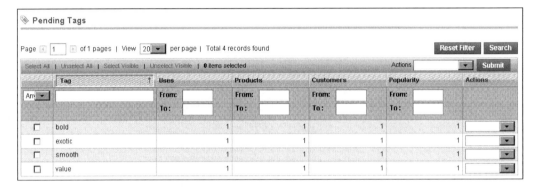

2. Select all of the tags that you want to approve or reject. Do this by enabling the checkbox at the beginning of the tag's line:

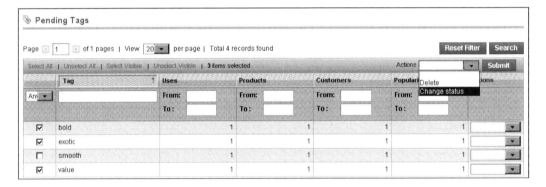

3. From the **Actions** drop-down menu, select **Change status**.

4. Another drop-down menu appears to the right of **Actions**. From that **Status** drop-down menu, select the new status for the selected tags.

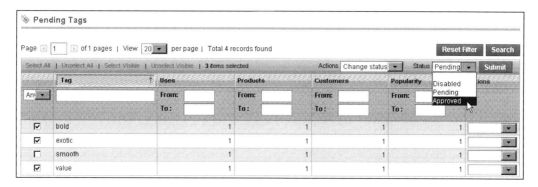

5. Click on the **Submit** button. The status of all the tags is changed.

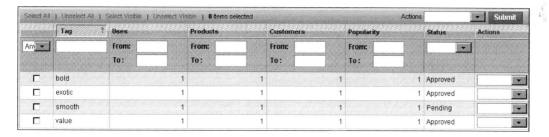

Once a tag is approved, it will be applied to the product(s) that customers assigned to the tag, and it will appear in the tag cloud. Only tags that are approved and that are applied to a product appear in the tag cloud.

Use the tag report to run a tagging contest

Magento's **Customers Tags** report can be used to run a contest where the customer who contributes the most tags wins a prize. The **Customers Tags** report shows you all of your logged-in customers and the number of tags they have created on your site:

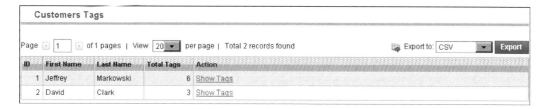

This report has some limitations that you must consider before using it to run a tagging contest. Let's discuss these limitations. Then, we'll go step-by-step through the process of running your tagging contest.

Limitations of the tagging report

First, notice that the report gives no dates for when the tags were submitted. However, if you click on the **Show Tags** link next to the customer's name, the report will show the tags submitted by that customer, including the dates they were submitted on:

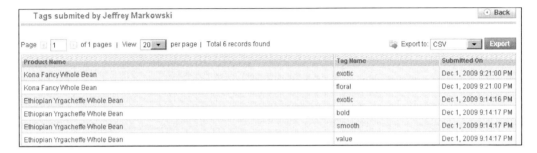

This means that if you want the dates that all the tags were submitted, you'll need to run the report for each customer who submitted tags. It takes only a few seconds per customer. However, if you have dozens (or hundreds) of customers submitting tags, then this could take hours.

Also notice the **Export** button on the upper-right hand side. This button exports only the data that you are looking at. If you are looking at the home page of this report, which shows only the customers and the number of tags submitted by each customer, then only that data will be exported. If you are looking at a report for a specific customer, which shows the tags and dates for that customer, then only that data will be exported.

The easiest way to run your tagging contest is to start the contest as soon as you enable tagging. That way, you will not need to filter out tags that customers added before your contest started. If you start the contest after customers have added tags, then you will need to run the report for each customer that added tags, export it to a spreadsheet, and filter out the tags created before the contest began.

How to do it...

1. If tagging is enabled in your store, then consider turning it off until the contest starts. See the *How to do it...* section of enabling or disabling tagging mentioned earlier in this chapter.

2. If your products have already been tagged, then consider deleting all of the tags. This will greatly simplify running the **Customer Tags** report. It will mean that you don't need to run the report for each customer because all customers will start at the same time, with the same number of tags (zero). See the *How to do it...* section within moderate (Approve or Reject) tags submitted by customers earlier in the chapter. In Step 3 of that procedure, from the **Action** drop-down menu, instead of selecting **Change status**, select **Delete**.

3. Customers will need to create new accounts to enter the contest. Consider requiring them to verify their e-mail addresses, so that you know you are collecting valid e-mail addresses. Do this under **System | Configuration | Customer Configuration | Require Emails Confirmation**.

4. Announce the tagging contest. You can do this on your site in several ways:

5. Create a special page just for the announcement and the contest rules. This will be a static page. See *Create a basic landing page* in Chapter 3.

6. Add the announcement to your category home pages. The announcement should have a link to the contest's static page, so that customers can see the rules of the contest. See *Add videos, links, and other HTML to product pages* in Chapter 4. You can use this technique to add the contest announcement to category and product pages.

7. Add the announcement to your store's front page. Do this under **CMS | Manage Pages | home**.

> Make sure the contest announcement specifies that your customer must log in or create an account on your site to enter. Only logged-in customers will get credit for their tags. One of the advantages for you will be while building your newsletter subscription because all of these new accounts will, by default, receive your newsletter.

8. On the day that you start your contest, enable tagging.

9. As the contest runs, consider updating the contest announcements with the number of tags submitted till date, the number of tags submitted by the customer who is in the lead, or the most imaginative tags submitted so far.

10. At the end of the contest, run the **Customer Tags** report. Because there were no tags in your store at the beginning of the contest, this report will contain an accurate count of all the tags ever submitted by each customer during the contest.

11. Announce the winner using the same methods that you used to announce the contest.

There's more...

The prize for your contest might be a gift certificate to your store. In Chapter 8, we cover creating a gift certificate.

Enabling e-mail to a friend

Magento enables shoppers on your site to send e-mails to their friends about your products:

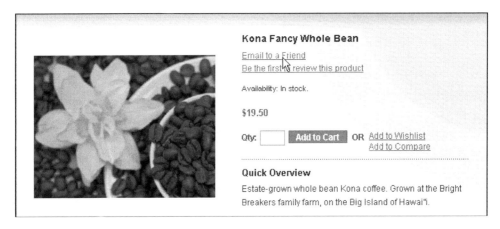

When the shopper clicks the **Email to a Friend** link, he/she is taken to a page where the shopper composes the e-mail:

The recipient will receive an e-mail with a link to the product and the shopper's message:

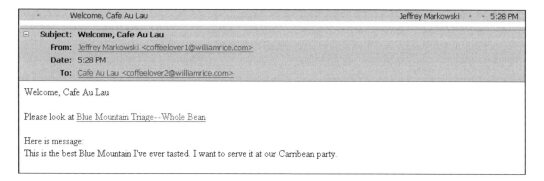

Notice that the message contains text that the shopper did not add. For example, the **Welcome**, **Please look at**... and **Here is message:** text. This text is in the e-mail template. You can customize that template for your store. You can change the text, add formatting, and add graphics.

How to do it...

Let's create a custom e-mail to a friend template. These directions are also found in Chapter 7, under *Customize transactional e-mails*.

1. In the admin interface, select **System | Transactional Emails**.

2. Select the **Add New Template** button. The **New Email Template** page displays:

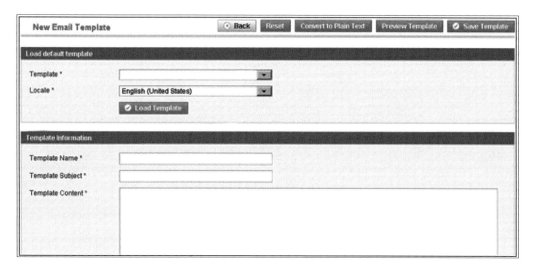

3. From the **Template** drop-down list, select **Send product to a friend**.

4. From the **Locale** drop-down list, select the language that you are using for your store.

5. Select the **Load Template** button. The standard e-mail template is loaded:

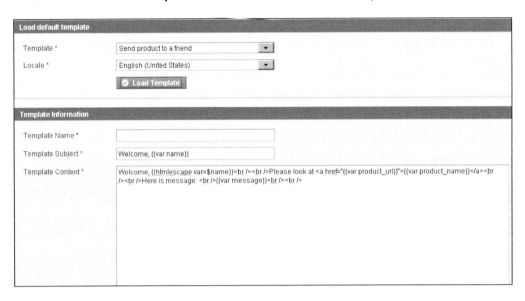

6. This is the default template. You will save this template under a different name and customize it with your store's information.

7. In **Template Name**, enter a prefix of your own, followed by the default name of the template. For example, **Customize: Send product to a friend**.

8. The **Template Content** is the body of the e-mail. This is what your customer receives.

9. Edit the **Template Subject** and **Template Content**. In the standard template, the following variables are used:

This variable...	...inserts this text into the e-mail...
`{{var name}}`	The name of the e-mail recipient, as entered by the customer who is sending the e-mail.
`{{var customer.name}}` and `{{var customer.store. name}}`	These insert the name of the sender and the name of your store. **These do not appear in the standard template**. However, if you wanted to add them to the message, then you could insert a line like this into the template: Dear `{{var name}}`, Your friend `{{var customer.name}}` wants you to take a look at this product, from `{{var customer. store.name}}`.

This variable...	...inserts this text into the e-mail...
`<a href="{{var product_url}}">{{var product_name}}</a>`	This inserts a link to the product. You almost certainly want to leave this in the e-mail template.
`{{var message}}`	This inserts the text of the message that the sender typed into the e-mail form.

10. Save the template.

11. Preview the template. If needed, make some more changes and save again.

How to do it...

Let's enable e-mail to a friend:

1. Select **System | Configuration | Email to a friend**. The settings for the **Email to a Friend** function displays:

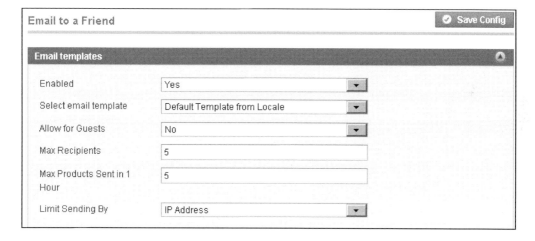

2. For **Enabled**, select **Yes**. This places the **Email to a Friend** link on the product page.

3. For **Select email template**, select the standard template or the customized one that you created.

4. For **Allow for Guests**, if you select **No**, then the e-mail link will appear only for customers who are logged into your store. If you select **Yes**, then the link will appear for all customers.

Some store owners use this to prevent their sites from being used to send spam. However, you can see that the settings for **Max Recipients**, **Max Products Sent in 1 Hour**, and **Limit Sending By** already help to prevent that. Consider setting **Allow for Guests** to **Yes** and allowing anonymous visitors to send e-mail to their friends about your products. If a spammer overcomes the other settings and uses your site to send spam, then you can try setting **Allow for Guests** to **No**.

5. When the customer sends the e-mail, he/she must enter the names and e-mail addresses of the recipients. **Max Recipients** sets the maximum number of recipients that the customer can specify for a message.

6. **Max Products Sent in 1 Hour** limits the number of products that the sender can send in one hour. The "sender" here is defined as the logged-in user, the IP address, or the cookie.

7. **Limit Sending By** determines if an anonymous visitor to your site is identified by their **IP address** or by a **Cookie** that Magento sets. For example, if you select **5** products for **Max Products Sent in 1 Hour** and **IP address** for **Limit Sending By**, then that means a single IP address can send only 5 e-mails in an hour. If you select **Cookie** for this setting, that means the browser with the cookie can send only 5 e-mails in one hour. **IP address** is safer than **Cookie** because some visitors might reject or clean their cookies.

8. Save the configuration.

9. Test the feature by sending an e-mail as both a logged-in user and an anonymous visitor.

There's more...

The instructions mentioned for creating a new e-mail template gave you two additional variables that you can use in the template. If you want a list of variables for e-mail templates, then search the official Magento site for "list of variables for mail template".

9

Internationalization

In this chapter, you will learn how to prepare your store for international sales. This chapter goes beyond just installing a new language pack. There are many other things that need to be considered, such as:

- ▶ Translating your products
- ▶ Creating a new URL for your international store
- ▶ Customizing transactional e-mails for your international store
- ▶ Translating CMS pages
- ▶ Creating a new website versus a new storefront

Internationalization is more than a new language

Magento gives you the ability to display your store in different languages. When you enable support for multiple languages, Magento will display the store navigation in the language that the shopper selects. Magento does this through language packs that you install.

However, Magento won't translate your product descriptions, category names, and other product information. You will need to translate the product information. Then, both the store navigation and the product information will be displayed in the language that the shopper selects.

Here is an example of a Magento store that was created in English. The store administrator installed the French language pack. Now, when the shopper selects the French language, Magento displays the navigation items in French. For example, the block labeled **MY CART** in English is now labeled **MON PANIER**. Magento did that with its French language pack:

However, the product information did not translate. The category names across the top are still in English. The sidebars and the ad in the top-center of the page are also still in English. These items are created by the store administrator. The store administrator did not create French versions of these items, so they aren't translated when the shopper chooses the French language.

Here is an example of a Magento store where both the interface and the product information have been translated into German:

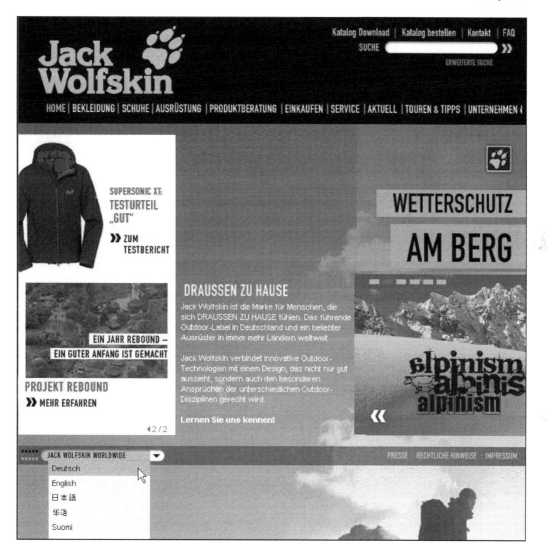

But as the title of this section states, internationalization is more than just enabling multiple languages. When you expand your Magento store into another country, you will probably need to change more than just the language. For example, let's look at the shopping cart for Jack Wolfskin's German store:

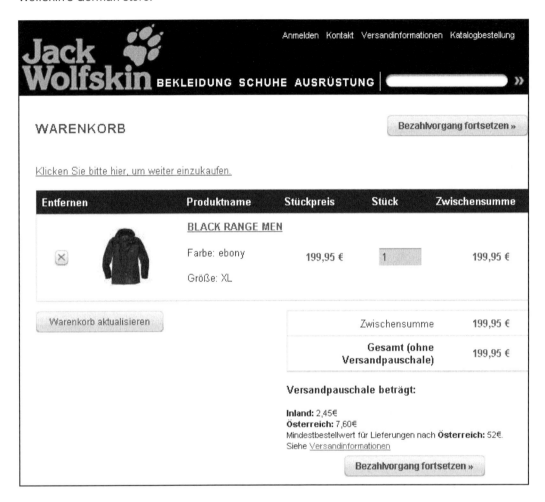

Notice that in the lower-right corner of the shopping cart, the cart displays shipping charges (**Versandpauschale beträgt:**). There is one charge for shipping in Germany (**Inland**) and another to Austria (**Österreich**). Moreover, there is a notice that a minimum purchase of 52 Euros is required to ship to Austria (**Mindestbestellwert für Lieferungen nach Österreich**).

While the customer is entering their payment information, they must select between Germany and Austria:

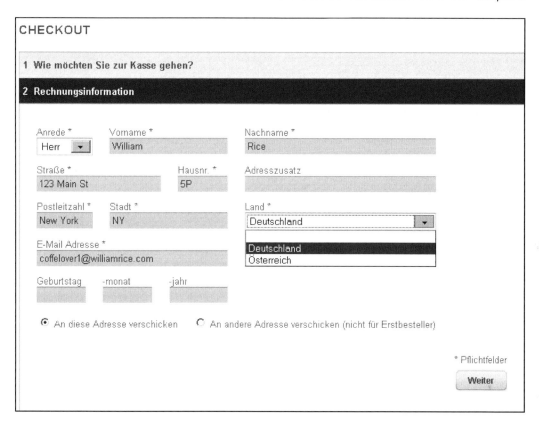

So we can see that there are some features in the German store that would not be in the English store: a notice in the shopping cart about shipping charges and minimum amounts for orders to Austria and a drop-down list of countries on the billing information page. Installing a language pack will not add these features.

Expanding your store into a new market might require you to do more than just translate it. That new market might have different laws, customs, and unique business situations that require you to enable and disable some of Magento's features. **Language packs only translate the Magento features that are already there in your store; they do not disable or enable Magento's features**. We will need to do something more than just translate our existing customer interface into a new language. We will need to create a new customer interface with its own unique features. We will do this by creating a new Magento website.

Website, store, store view: What's the difference?

Before we create a new store for our international audience, we need to learn some Magento terminology. Understand that Magento uses the terms website, store, and store view differently than we do in casual conversation.

If your customer is looking at your online store, he/she is looking at a **store view**. A store view is the presentation of a store. When a customer chooses a language or store from Magento's drop-down list, that customer is really selecting a store view.

A store without a store view can never be viewed by your customers. Changing the store view is not intended to change the content of the store that the shopper sees. Instead, it changes just the wording, images, and/or design.

Behind every store view is a store. In Magento, a store is defined as a collection of products that are all under the same root category. In the following screenshot, the store views **Brew-Me-A-Cup** and **Brew-Me-A-Pot** are both under the store labeled **Main Website Store**:

There is also a store called **En Espanol**. Like **Main Website Store**, **En Espanol** is under **Main Website**. This means that both **Main Website Store** and **En Espanol** have access to the same product categories. In this case, both of them have access to all the products from the category **Default Category**:

Of course, the store **En Espanol** has a store view so that the customer can select it.

As stated earlier, a store view is the presentation for a store. If you're selling the same merchandise to the same type of customer, and if you're using the same billing and shipping methods, but a different language, then the usual solution is to make one store with a different store view for each language. For example, if you're selling to customers in Quebec, where both English and French are the official languages, you might want one store with a store view in English and another with a store view in French.

However, if you're selling different merchandise to the same customers, and if you're using the same billing and shipping methods, then the usual solution is to create a store for each type of merchandise. For example, if you sell electronics online, and if you decide to also sell appliances, then you might create another store for the appliances. Of course, you would also create a store view for the appliances.

When you expand into another country, you might be able to get away with just creating a store view in another language. However, expanding into an international market often requires more than just another language. It can also require different billing methods, shipping methods, and shipping information. It can also require that you remove some products or categories from the store or change the organization of the categories. Depending upon local law, you might also need to include additional information pages such as privacy conditions or business licenses. You cannot make these kinds of structural changes with a store or store view. Instead, you must create a separate website.

In Magento, all of the stores under a website must share the same customer information, shopping cart, inventory, billing methods, and shipping methods. If any of these things must change for your international market, then just creating a new store will not suffice. Instead, you must create a new website.

A single Magneto installation can be used to manage multiple websites. These websites can have different customer information, shopping cart, inventory, billing methods, and shipping methods or they can be the same. Different websites can have different URLs or share the same web address.

 Some Magento experts recommend that when you expand into a new market, you create a new store view for the new language. I am recommending that you create a new website. However, the store view opinion is so pervasive that you should investigate it. Your decision is this: Create a new website, or a new store under the original website.

Installing a language pack

Installing a language pack is the first step to internationalizing your store. Remember, the language pack will translate Magento's interface, not your product information.

How to do it....

First, we need to get the extension key for the language pack.

1. Point your browser to `http://www.magentocommerce.com/magento-connect`.
2. Search for the language pack of your choice:

3. Click the link for **Get extension key**.

4. You will be prompted to agree to the extension license agreement:

5. Click on the **GET EXTENSION KEY** button. The extension key is displayed:

6. Select and copy the extension key. You might want to keep this window open while you complete the next part.

Now, it is time to install the extension:

1. In another browser tab or window, log in to the administrative interface of your Magento.

2. Select **System | Magento Connect | Magento Connect Manager**.

3. You will be prompted to log in to the connect manager. Enter your Magento administrator username and password, and click on the **Log In** button:

4. Paste the extension key into the field provided on the page:

5. Click on the **Install** button.
6. The bottom of the page will display the installation's progress.

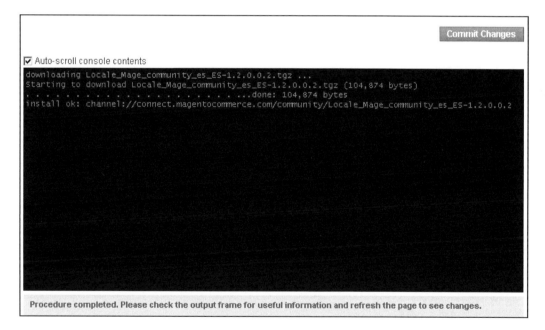

7. When the system tells you that the installation is complete, click on the **Refresh** button at the bottom of the page. Magento will display the module that you just installed:

8. At the top of the page, click on the **Return to Admin** link.

Now let's check to ensure that the language pack is really installed:

1. Select **System | Configuration**.

2. Under **General**, select **Locale Options**.

3. In the drop-down field for **Locale**, look for the name of the language pack that you just installed. It should be there.

4. Leave this page without saving. You don't want to change the language yet!

There's more...

The language pack will translate your interface. Eventually, you will need to translate your product information. But before you do that, you will need to create a new website/store/store view for the new language.

Creating a new website/store/store view

In this section, you will create a new website. In the next section, you will put that website under a different URL on your server.

How to do it....

1. From the administrative interface, select **System | Manage Stores**.

2. Click on the **Create Website** button. The **New Website** page displays. There are only three fields on this page that you need to enter.

3. Enter a **Name** for the website. This is the name that you will see in the administrative interface. Your customers will never see this name. It should be meaningful to you.

4. Enter a **Code** for the website. It must consist of only letters and numbers, with no spaces. This is the code that Magento will use for the website.

5. The **Sort Order** determines the order of this website in drop-down lists.

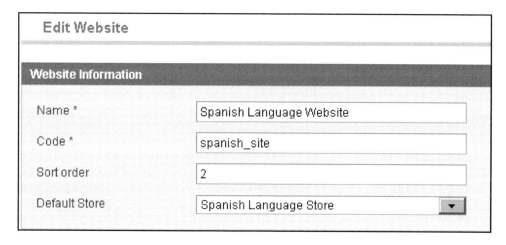

6. Save the website. You are returned to the **Manage Stores** page.

7. Click on the **Create Store** button.

8. For **Website**, select the website that you just created.

9. Give the store a **Name**. Only you will see this name.

10. For **Default Category**, leave the setting at the default root category.

11. Save the store. You are returned to the **Manage Stores** page.

12. Click on the **Create Store View** button.

13. For **Store**, select the store that you just created.

14. For **Name**, enter the name that you want your customers to see. Think about what you are asking your customer. Are you asking them to select their language, for example, "Espanol" or "Deutch", or are you asking them to select their country, for example, "Spain" or "Deutchland".

15. Enter a **Code** for the store view. It must consist of only letters and numbers, with no spaces. This is the code that Magento will use for the store view.

16. The **Sort Order** determines the order of this store view in drop-down lists. Your customers will see this drop-down list. Remember, when a customer selects a store or language, they are really selecting a store view.

17. For **Status**, leave it at **Disabled** until you are ready to introduce your store. Then you can set it to **Enabled**.

18. Save the store view.

Website Name	Store Name	Store View Name
Manage Stores		⊕ Create Website ⊕ Create St
Page [ ] 1 [ ] of 1 pages	View 20 ▼ per page	Total 3 records found		
Main Website	Main Website Store	Brew-Me-A-Cup
Main Website	Main Website Store	Brew-Me-A-Pot
Spanish Language Website	Spanish Language Store	Spain

There's more...

Now, you are ready to configure your international website/store/store view.

Setting up your international website/store/store view under a separate URL

For our example store, we use `http://brew-me-a-cup.com`. We are going to set up our store for Spain under `http://brew-me-a-cup.com/spain`. However, we must be careful from now on to ensure that we never have a product or category that uses the URL `/spain`. That URL is now reserved only for our Spanish customers.

How to do it....

First, we will copy `.htaccess` and `index.php` into the new website's directory.

1. On your web server, under the default Magento directory, create another directory for your international store. In our example, we will create `http://brew-me-a-cup.com/spain`.

2. From the default Magento directory, copy the files `.htaccess` and `index.php` into the directory that you just created.

3. With a text editor, open the copy of `index.php`.

4. Look for the line `$mageFilename = 'app/Mage.php';`. Change it to `$mageFilename = '../app/Mage.php';`.

5. Look for the line `Mage::run();`. In the parentheses, insert the code for the website that you created. In our example, it will read `Mage::run('spanish_site','website');`. Notice the single quotes and the addition of the word `'website'`. These are required.

6. Save the file.

Now, let's configure the website in Magento.

1. Switch to your browser and log in to the Magento administrative interface.
2. Select **System | Configuration**.
3. From the **Current Configuration Scope:** drop-down list, select the international website that you created earlier:

4. Select the **General** option under the **GENERAL** tab:

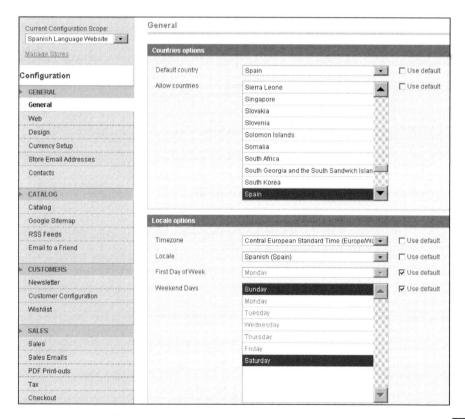

5. Since this website is for another country, you will probably want to change the settings for **Default country.**

   Next to the setting, click to remove the check mark for **Use default**.

   Select a new **Default country**.

6. For **Locale**, select the language pack that you installed earlier:

   Next to the setting, click to remove the check mark for **Use default**.

   Select a new **Locale**.

7. Change the other settings under this tab as needed.

8. Save.

9. Select the **General** tab. You will see the URL settings for this website. At this time, they are all set to the default URL:

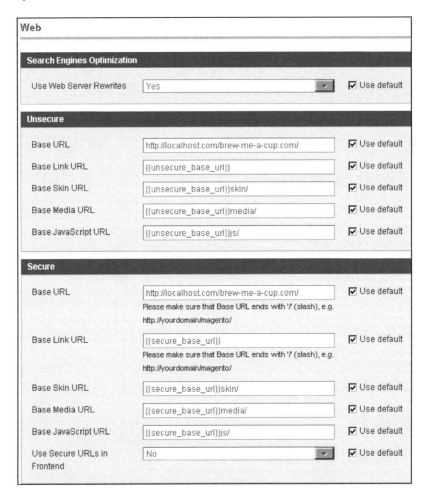

Because you put the international store under a different URL, you will need to change many of these URL settings.

10. For **Base URL**, enter the web address of the international store. In our example store, we would use `http://brew-me-a-cup.com/spain/`.

11. You can leave **Base Link URL** as it is.

12. For **Base Skin URL**, **Base Media URL**, and **Base JavaScript URL**, you will need to enter the path to the original store's directories. In our example store, we would use `http://brew-me-a-cup.com/skin`, `http://brew-me-a-cup.com/media` and `http://brew-me-a-cup.com/js`.

   If you want to create a separate skin for your international store or use a separate media or JavaScript directory, then you would enter the paths to those directories. Because those are beyond the scope of this book, we are using the original store's directories.

13. Select **Catalog | Price**.

14. For **Catalog Price Scope**, select **Website**. This enables you to set a different price for the same product in your international store. If you leave this setting at the default of **Global**, you will be forced to charge the same price for a product in all of your websites.

15. Select the **Customer Configuration** tab.

16. Select the **Account Sharing Options** section.

17. For **Share Customer Accounts**, select either **Global** or **Per Website**. If you want to share customer accounts among all your websites, then select **Global**. If you want to separate customer accounts, so that they do not cross over from one website to another, then select **Per Website**.

18. For the new website, you should also configure the Tax, Shipping Settings, Shipping Methods, and Payment Methods. When configuring each of these, make sure that you have the website selected as the Current Configuration Scope.

19. Save the configuration.

20. Test your new store. Navigate to the URL for the frontend of the new store. You should see a page which has all the same content and design as the original store, but the Magento navigation elements and the block title should be translated:

Enabling and translating your products for the international store view

If you are viewing your international store, then you might see the same catalog of products as your original store. Alternatively, the store might not have any products right now.

If you see the same products, this is because the international website and the original website use the same root category and your products are enabled for all store views. Remember, the root category is the top-most category in your catalog. When you select a root category for a website, you are making all of the categories and products under it available to the website.

If the catalog in the international website is blank (you are showing no products), then it is because the products are not enabled for your international website.

How to do it....

Firstly, you need to enable the product for the international website.

1. From the Magento administrative interface, select **Catalog | Manage Products**.

2. Select a product from your catalog.

3. Select the **Websites** tab. You will see the default website and the international website that you created:

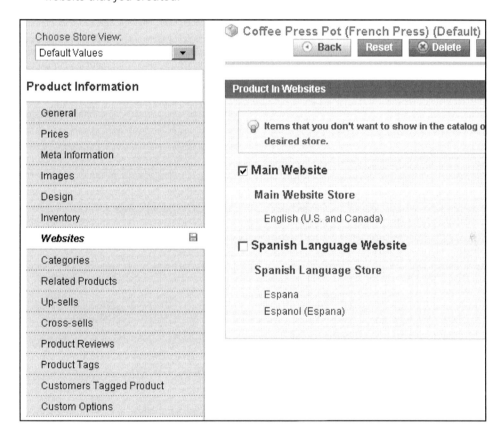

4. Click to place a check mark in the box for the international website.

5. Click on the **Save and Continue Edit** button.

Now, translate the product description.

1. Select the **General** tab.

2. From the **Choose Store View** menu, select the store view for your international storefront.

3. Next to **Name**, **Description**, and **Short Description**, you will see checkboxes for **Use Default Value**. Remove the check marks from these.

4. Enter the translations for **Name**, **Description**, and **Short Description**:

5. Change any other fields under this tab that fit your business model. For example:

   If you want this product to be displayed as a "**New Product**" on the international website, then you can change the fields for **Set Product** as **New**.

6. Using the **Status** setting, you can enable or disable this product for each website. You can set the **Visibility** for this product in each website.

7. Some settings cannot be changed because they are global such as the **SKU** and **Weight**.

8. Click on the **Save and Continue Edit** button.

At this point, edit the remaining tabs. Some of the remaining tabs contain settings that you can edit for your international website or store view. Let's list the tabs and discuss the options for them.

Prices tab

The only settings in this tab that is always global—that you cannot change for each website—is the **Google Checkout** setting. All of the other settings can be changed per website (see steps 15 to 17 in the *How to do it...* section under Set up your international website/store/store view under a separate URL)

Meta information

If you plan to submit this website to a foreign-language search engine, then consider adding meta information in that language.

Images

Images can be specified per store view. If customizing the product image for the culture that you are selling to will help sales, then you can upload images just for the selected store view.

Inventory

All inventory settings are global. If you need different inventory settings for different stores, then you must create a duplicate product with a different SKU.

Categories

When you created your international store, you selected a root category for that store. Selecting a store view from the **Choose Store View** menu will show just the categories that apply to that store view.

Related products, up-sells, cross-sells

These settings can be global or per store view. If you associate a product with the one you've translated, remember to also translate the associated product.

Product reviews, product tags, customer tagged products

If your international store uses a different language to your original store, then you probably will want to make these apply to just one store view. If you make them global, then shoppers will see reviews and tags in different languages.

Custom options

These can be set per store view or globally. Now save and test your changes.
Save the product.

1. Test the product in your store's frontend.

2. Repeat as needed for each product in your international store.

Translating CMS pages (Front page, About Us, Customer Service, and so on)

You probably want the front page of your international website to appear in your customers' native language. You will need to translate this page. You will also need to translate the **About Us**, **Customer Service**, and other static pages. In the following screenshot, you can see that we added a CMS front page for our Spanish store view:

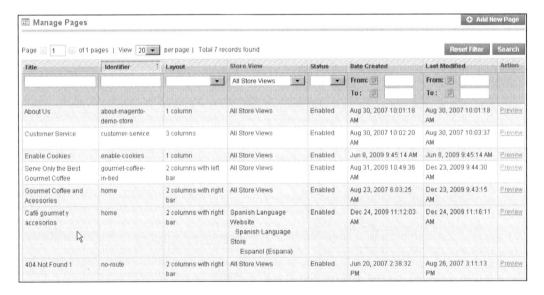

The result is a front page that is unique to this international store view:

How to do it...

1. From the administrative interface, select **CMS | Manage Pages**.

2. Add a new static page. Use the procedure in *Create a basic landing page* in Chapter 3.

3. For the page's **Store View**, select your international storefront.

4. For the page's **Identifier**, leave it the same as the original store. For example, the front page of the website will be **home** for both the original and international store views:

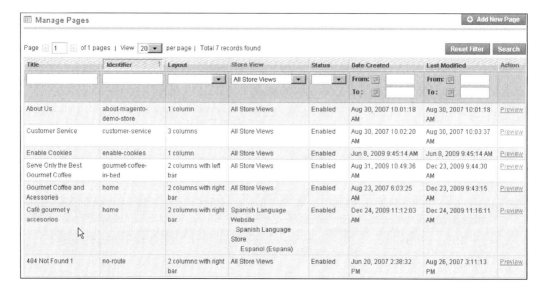

5. Remember to **Enable** the page.

6. Save the CMS page.

7. Repeat this for each of the CMS pages that you need for your international store:

   ❑ **About Us**

   ❑ **Customer Service**

   ❑ **Enable Cookies**

   ❑ **Home Page**

   ❑ **404 Not Found**

How it works...

When a visitor to your international storefront requests a CMS page, Magento will serve the translated page specified for that website instead of the main website.

Translating transactional e-mails

In Chapter 7, you saw how to customize transactional e-mails. This was covered in the section *Customizing transactional e-mails*. Now, you must translate those e-mails for your international website. If you don't translate the transactional e-mails, then you will be sending order confirmations, shipping notices, and other e-mails to your customers that are not written in their language.

How to do it...

1. In the admin interface, select **System |Transactional Emails**.

2. Select the **Add New Template** button. The **New Email Template** page displays:

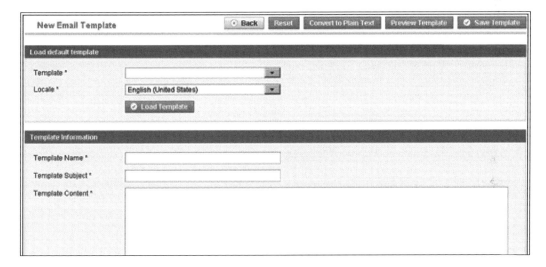

3. From the **Template** drop-down list, select the first e-mail template that you need to translate. For example, you probably do not need to translate the template **New admin password**.

4. From the **Locale** drop-down list, select the language that you are using for your international storefront.

   This step is crucial. By selecting a **Locale** for this template, you are enabling this template for any website or store view that uses the Locale.

5. Select the **Load Template** button.

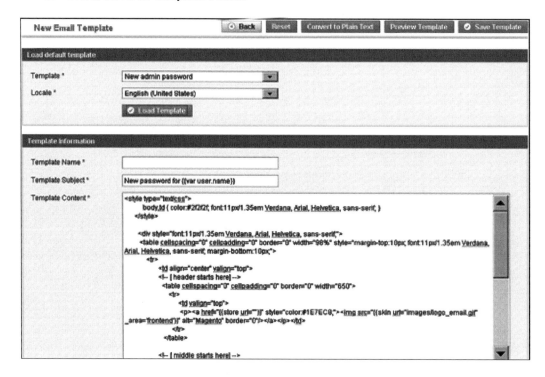

The default template for this type of e-mail will load. Even though you might have selected a non-English language, you will see that the template is written in English. You will save this template under a different name, and customize it with your store's information.

6. In **Template Name**, enter a prefix of your own, followed by the default name of the template. For example, **Spanish: New Order**.

   The **Template Content** is the body of the e-mail. This is what your customer receives. You must replace the default, fictional information in the body with your store's information. The easiest way to do this is to copy the code out of the **Template Content**, paste it into a word processor, use **Find and Replace** to replace the fictional information, and then copy-and-paste it back into Magento.

7. Click in the **Template Content**.

8. From your browser's **Edit** menu, select **Select All**.

9. From your browser's **Edit** menu, select **Copy**.

10. Launch your favorite word processor, like WordPad or Text Editor.

11. In a blank document, paste the code that you copied out of the **Template Content**.

12. Use your word processor's **Find and Replace** function to:

Find this text...	...and replace it with this text...
alt="Magento"	alt="Your Store's Name" (where Your Store's Name is the name of your store).
Magento Demo Store	The name of your store.
mailto:magento@varien.com	mailto:your store's email address (where your store's email address is the e-mail address of your store)
dummyemail@magentocommerce.com	mailto:your store's email address (where your store's email address is the e-mail address of your store)
(800) DEMO-STORE	The phone number of your store.
Monday - Friday, 8am - 5pm PST	Your store's customer service hours.

13. Once again, use **Edit | Select All** to select all of the text in the word processor.

14. Switch over to Magento.

15. Delete the existing **Template Content**.

16. Paste the text that you edited.

17. Save the template.

18. Preview the template. If needed, make more changes and save again.

Repeat this for each e-mail template that your international customers will receive.

Setting the currency for your international store

Unless you chose multiple currencies for your original store, your international store is still using your home currency. You can change this so that prices are displayed in the currency used by your international customers.

How to do it...

1. Select **System | Configuration | Currency Setup**.

2. From the **Current Configuration Scope** drop-down menu, select your international website or your international store view.

3. For the **Base currency** and **Default display currency**, disable the check mark from **Use default**. Then, select the currency for the international store:

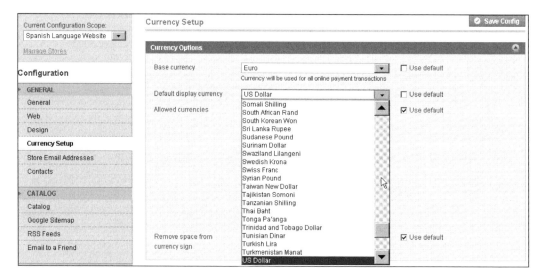

4. Save the configuration.

Having a grand opening sale for your international storefront

Catalog Price Rules and **Shopping Cart Price Rules** are as per website. While creating a rule, you select the website(s) to which you want the rule to apply. You can use a catalog price rule to hold a special sale for your international store.

How to do it...

1. From the administrative interface, select **Promotions | Catalog Price Rules**.

2. Create a new rule.

3. Under the **Rule Information** tab for **Websites**, select your international website.

4. Finish the rule, as described under *Create a catalog price rule* in Chapter 6.

How it works...

Because rules are applied to an entire website and all of the stores under that site, we created a separate site for your international store. This enabled you to create rules just for your international store.

.

10

Create a Wholesale Store

In this chapter, you will learn how to create a wholesale store. This store will be open only to wholesale customers. It will be for business-to-business sales only.

The customers are the difference

What is the difference between a wholesale store and a retail store? The answer can be different for the customer and for the store owner. The customer's answer might be something like this:

- ▶ I don't pay sales tax.
- ▶ I must buy larger quantities, but in exchange I get lower prices.
- ▶ Gift wrapping and shipping to multiple locations are almost never available, but once again, in exchange I get lower prices.
- ▶ I must present documentation to the store that I am a legitimate wholesale customer such as a certificate that shows I am exempt from sales taxes or a business license.

Each of these points must be addressed in your Magento store.

From the store owner's point of view, the main difference between a wholesale and retail store is this:

Wholesale customers are a different type of customers.

If that statement makes you think, "I should create a customer group just for my wholesale customers", then you are thinking like a Magento store owner. We will talk more about that later.

Using the same storefront for wholesale and retail customers

The standard, open-source Magento system cannot show or hide products, based upon the customer type. This can be accomplished with an add-on. However, we will accomplish building a wholesale store with the standard Magento installation.

If you use the same storefront for both wholesale and retail customers, you will be forced to show them the same products. However, you do not need to show them the same prices. That is because Magento can change the prices in your catalog based upon the type of customer that is logged in.

In the *Magento Beginner's Guide*, we showed you how to create customer groups, and how to assign a customer to a customer group. In this chapter, we will combine those techniques to create wholesale customers.

Wholesale customers usually don't pay sales tax. Sales tax can be removed using a shopping cart price rule. We showed you how to create this in Chapter 6. In this chapter, we will show you how to create a shopping cart price rule that removes sales taxes for wholesale customers.

You should also create a static page, or CMS page, explaining the conditions for becoming a wholesale customer. For example, you will probably require the customer to fax or e-mail a certificate that exempts them from paying sales tax or a business license. In Chapter 3, under *Create a basic landing page*, we showed you how to create a CMS page.

Finally, you might want to announce that you have wholesale prices available. You can do this by adding a static block to each page in your catalog. This static block consists of content that will be displayed in the sidebar of every page of your site. We will cover that technique in this chapter.

 Adding a static block is an especially useful technique. You can use the static block to announce anything about your store: special deals, promotions, awards, contests, and more.

So now, to create a wholesale version of our store, we will combine these techniques:

1. Create a CMS page explaining the requirements for becoming a wholesale customer.
2. Add a static block advertising our wholesale option, and add it to our catalog pages:

   Create a static block.

   Add the static block to the catalog pages.
3. Create a customer group for wholesale customers.
4. Assign customers to the wholesale group.

5. Create a shopping cart price rule that removes sales taxes for wholesale customers.

6. Assign various levels of discounts to our products for wholesale customers, when those products are purchased in large quantities.

7. Profit!

As you can see, creating a wholesale version of your store requires more than just creating a customer group called "Wholesale".

Creating a CMS page explaining conditions for becoming a wholesale customer

In Chapter 3, under *Create a basic landing page*, we showed you how to create a CMS page. If you are going to attract wholesale customers, then consider creating a CMS page to explain the process of becoming a wholesale customer.

How to do it...

1. Log in to your site's backend or Administrative Panel.

2. Select **CMS | Manage Pages**. The **Manage Pages** page displays. A list of the CMS pages (or "static pages") in your store should appear on this page.

3. Select the **Add New Page** button.

4. The **Edit Page** will display. The **General Information** tab is selected for you.

5. Enter a **Page Title**. This will appear in the visitor's browser title bar. For example, you could use **How to Become a Wholesale Customer**.

6. Enter an **SEF URL Identifier**. This will be added to your domain name to form the URL of the page. For example, you could use `wholesale-customers`, so the URL of our page will be `http://brew-me-a-cup.com/wholesale-customers`.

7. To activate this page, under **Status**, select **Enabled**.

8. In the **Content** field, enter the HTML code for this page. This is just like creating any web page. Here is one method:

   Open a web page editor. Almost any basic HTML editor will suffice.

   Write the web page.

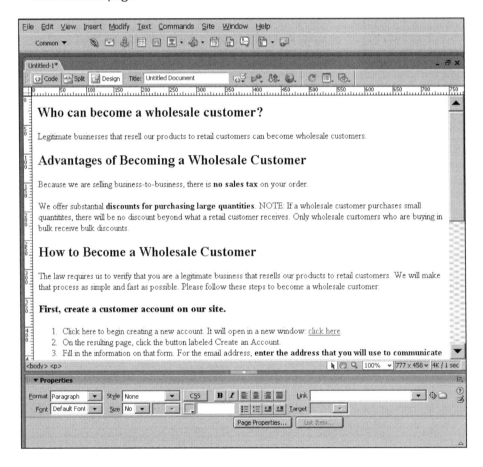

9. Switch to the **Code** view in your web page editor, so that you are looking at the HTML code for the page that you wrote:

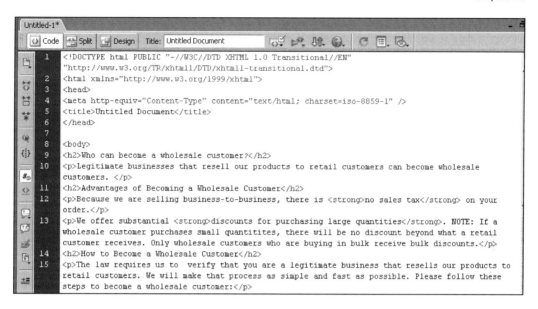

10. Select and copy the text that you wrote. This will be everything in between the `<body>` and `</body>` tags.

11. Switch back to Magento.

12. Paste the text into the **Content** field.

13. Click on the **Save and Continue Edit** button.

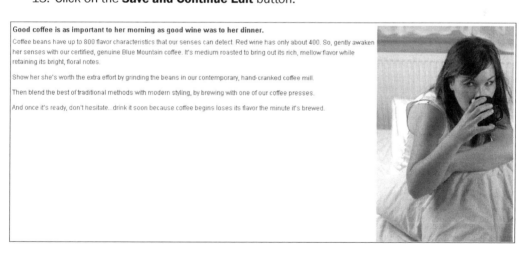

14. Select the **Custom Design** tab.

15. If you are using a custom theme, then from the **Custom Theme** drop-down list, select the name of that theme.

16. From the **Layout** drop-down list, select the type of layout that you want for this static page. In our example, we selected **2 columns with left bar**.

17. Save your work and preview the page:

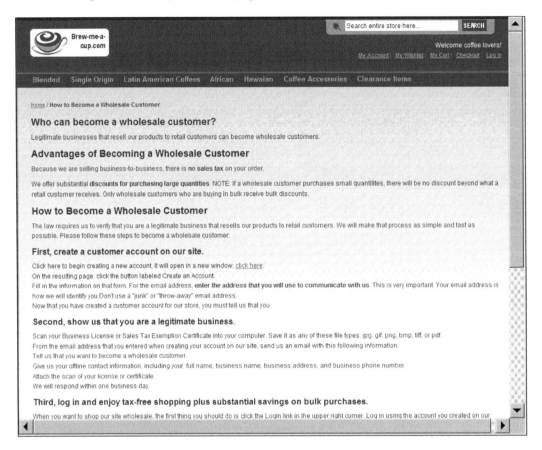

Creating a static block, and adding it to your catalog pages

A static block is a portable piece of HTML code that you can place anywhere in a page or site. You can put anything in a static block that you can put on a web page, if it fits the small space. Usually, you place a static block in the left or right column of a page. Sometimes you place it in a footer or header.

In our example, we will create a static block to inform shoppers of our wholesale program. However, you can use a static block for many other purposes such as to advertise sales, announce contests, feature products, and more.

How to do it...

You are about to create a new theme. Your store's layout, terminology, color scheme, typestyles, and images are controlled by its theme. Creating an entirely new theme for your site is beyond the scope of this book. Covering that requires an entire book by itself such as the *Magento Designer's Guide* from Packt.

However, in this procedure, we will create a new theme with one file—the catalog layout page. We will customize that one page. Magento will use the default theme for every other page in your store, except the one that we customize. This will give you some practice with themes, and help you decide if you want to delve into customizing themes.

1. First, let's create the new theme. Assuming that you are using the default Magento theme, find the file:

    `\app\design\frontend\default\default\layout\wishlist\catalog.xml`. You don't need to do anything with it yet. Just find it and make sure that you have access to it.

2. Create a new directory to hold the new theme. In our example store, we use a theme called `coffee`. So, we created this directory structure:

    `\app\design\frontend\default\coffee\layout\`.

    Notice that we needed to create an entire directory structure. Under `\app\design\frontend\default`, we created a new directory with our theme name `coffee`. Then, under `coffee`, we created the directory `layout`.

3. Copy the file `catalog.xml` from the directory you looked at in Step 1, to the directory that you just created.

Now, we create a new static block.

1. Log in to your site's backend or Administrative Panel.

2. Select **CMS | Static Blocks**. The **Manage Pages** page displays. A list of the CMS pages (or "static pages") in your store should appear on this page.

3. Select the **Add New Block** button. The **New Block** page will display.

4. In the **Block Title** field, enter a title for the block. Your customers will not see this title. However, you will see it in the list of static blocks.

5. In the **Identifier** field, enter a name for the block that consists of only letters, numbers, hyphens, and underscores. You will use this identifier later, when you modify the catalog.xml file that you copied in the previous part. If needed, write down this identifier so you remember it.

6. Select the **Store View**(s) for which this block is available. For this block to appear, it will need to be available to the store view, and it will need to be in the XML file for that store.

7. For **Status**, select **Enabled**.

8. In the **Content** field, enter the HTML code that will be displayed in the block. This can be text only or include a graphic. Remember that the block is small, so keep any graphics small and your text brief. In our example, we include a link to the CMS page that we created called, "How to Become a Wholesale Customer?":

9. Save the block.

Now, we edit the layout file so that it displays our static block.

1. Open catalog.xml in a text editor or an HTML editor.

2. Scroll down to the section of the file that controls the layout for the type of page that you want to modify.

If you want to modify...	Scroll down until you see this...

category and product pages	```<!--```
	
	```Default layout, loads most of the pages```
	
	```-->```
	
	```<default>```

just category landing pages	```<!--```
	
	```Category default layout```
	
	```-->```
	
	```<catalog_category_default>```

just product pages	```<!--```
	
	```Product view```
	
	```-->```
	
	```<catalog_product_view>```

3. To place the block in the left column, look for this code: `<reference name="left">`. To place it in the right column, look for `<reference name="right">`.

4. Add the code to display the static block. In our example, we have made the code we added **bold**. The name of our block is `are_you_wholesale`. Replace that with the name of the block that you created:

```
<default>
  <!-- Mage_Catalog -->

  <reference name="top.menu">
    <block type="catalog/navigation" name="catalog.topnav"
      template="catalog/navigation/top.phtml"/>
  </reference>

  <reference name="left">
    <block type="core/template" name="left.permanent.callout"
      template="callouts/left_col.phtml">
    <action method="setImgSrc"><src>images/media/
      col_left_callout.jpg</src></action>
    <action method="setImgAlt" translate="alt"
      module="catalog"><alt>Not sure what to order?. Call us at
      (555) 555-1212.</alt></action>
    <action method="setLinkUrl"><url>contacts</url></action>
```

```
      </block>
    </reference>

    <reference name="right">
      <block type="cms/block" name="are_you_wholesale">
        <action method="setBlockId"><block_id>are_you_wholesale
          </block_id></action>
      </block>
      <block type="core/template" before="cart_sidebar"
        name="catalog.compare.sidebar"
        template="catalog/product/compare/sidebar.phtml"/>
        <block type="core/template" name="right.permanent.callout"
          template="callouts/right_col.phtml"/>
    </reference>

    <reference name="footer_links">
      <action method="addLink" translate="label title"
module="catalog"
        ifconfig="catalog/seo/site_map"><label>Site Map</label><url
        helper="catalog/map/getCategoryUrl" /><title>Site
        Map</title></action>
    </reference>

  </default>
```

5. Save the file.

6. Select **System | Cache Management**.

7. From the **All Cache** drop-down menu, select **Disable**.

8. Save the cache settings.

9. Preview your site:

There's more...

You now have a static block that announces your wholesale customer option. You also have a CMS page explaining how to become a wholesale customer. Now, customers can and might begin sending you requests to be wholesale customers. The next technique deals with creating a wholesale customer group and assigning customers to that group.

Creating a customer group and assigning customers to the wholesale group

This procedure assumes that your customers have:

▸ Created customer accounts on your site.

▸ Emailed or faxed you the documents required to verify that they are wholesale customers.

How to do it...

First, create the customer group that we will use for our wholesale customers.

1. Log in to your site's backend or Administrative Panel.

2. Select **Customers | Customer Groups**.

3. Click on the **Add New Customer Group** button. The **New Customer Group** name page displays. There are only two fields that you need to complete.

4. For **Group Name**, enter **wholesale**.

5. For **Tax class**, select **Business customer**.

6. Save the group.

Now that we created the customer group, let's assign a customer to that group.

This procedure assumes that you know the e-mail address of the customer that you need to assign to the group. You can also search for the customer using their name, telephone number, zip code, country, and/or state.

1. Select **Customers | Manage Customers**.

2. In the shaded bar at the top of the customer list, in the **Email** field, enter the e-mail address of the customer that you want to assign:

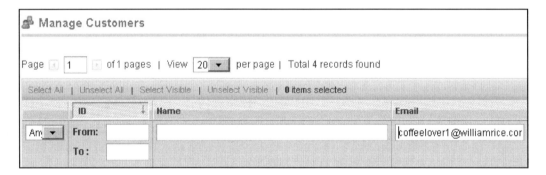

3. Click on the **Search** button. The customer record displays:

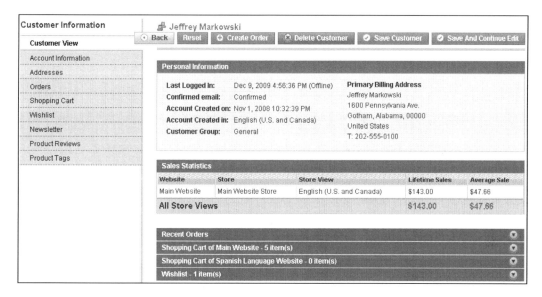

4. Select the **Account Information** tab.

5. From the **Customer Group** drop-down list, select **Wholesale**.

6. You might also want to enter the customer's Tax/VAT number in the field provided.

7. Save the customer.

Creating a tax rule that removes sales taxes for wholesale customers

Wholesale customers usually don't pay sales tax. Let's create a rule that removes the tax for wholesale customers only.

How to do it...

1. Log in to your site's backend or Administrative Panel.

2. Select **Sales | Tax | Customer Tax Classes**.

3. If you don't already have a wholesale customer tax class, then click the **Add New** button.

4. In the resulting page, for **Class Name**, enter **Wholesale**.

5. Click on the **Save Class** button. You are returned to the **Customer Tax Classes** page. You should see the Wholesale customer class that you just created.

6. Select **Sales | Tax | Manage Tax Zones and Rates**.

7. Click on the **Add New Tax Rate** button. The **New Tax Rate** page displays.

8. For **Tax Identifier**, enter a name that will describe this rule's purpose. For our example, we used **wholesale-no-tax-United-States**.

9. For **Country**, enter the country to which this rule will apply. At this time, you can have a rule apply to only one country. So if you have wholesale customers in several countries, you will need to create a rate for each country.

10. For **State** and **Zip/Post Code**, leave an asterisk in the field.

11. For **Rate**, leave it at zero.

12. Click on the **Save Rate** button.

13. Select **Sales | Tax | Manage Tax Rules**.

14. Click on the **Add New Tax Rule** button. The **New Rule** page displays.

15. Enter the **Name**. Your customers will never see this. This is only so that the site administrator (you) can identify the rule in a list. Make it descriptive so that you know what the rule does from the name. In our example, we use **Wholesale Customer No Sales Tax**.

16. For **Customer Tax Class,** select **Wholesale**.

17. For **Product Tax Class,** select all of the available product classes. This will remove sales tax for everything that wholesale customers buy.

Make sure that this is appropriate for your business. If you need to charge tax on certain kinds of products or services, even for wholesale customers, then you will need to create a product tax class for that type of product, and exclude it from this tax rule.

18. For **Tax Rate,** select the rate that you created above. In our example, we used **wholesale-no-tax-United-States**.

19. For **Priority** and **Sort Order**, enter **1**.

20. Save the rule. You will be returned to the **Manage Tax Rules** page.

There's more...

At the end of this procedure, you are on the **Manage Tax Rules** page. You can see a list of all the tax rules in your Magento store(s). It would be a good idea for you to click on each rule and see if it also applies to the wholesale customer group. You want to make sure that you know all of the tax rules that apply to each customer group. This is not a screen that you visit frequently. So, when you change or add a tax rule, it's usually a good idea to look at the other rules you have in effect, to see if any of them overlap.

Check your shopping cart price rules

You might have several shopping cart price rules that are effective, at the same time. For example, you might offer free shipping on orders over a specific amount, plus a coupon code, plus a discount if the customer buys specific items together. Usually, when you have multiple shopping cart rules, they apply only to retail customers. This is because wholesale customers are already receiving discounts for buying in bulk.

Now that you are dealing with wholesale customers, check each of your shopping cart price rules to see if it applies to wholesale customers. Make sure that you are not accidentally applying any rules that you do not want.

Do this under **Promotions | Shopping Care Price Rules**.

Creating quantity discounts for wholesale customers

In this section, we will look at two ways to apply a quantity discount to products for the wholesale customer group. We will see how to apply tiered pricing and a catalog price rule.

Tiered pricing

To create a discount for buying more than one of a product, you usually use the tiered pricing feature. For example, these settings:

Produce this result:

Ethiopian Yrgacheffe Whole Bean

★★★★★ 1 Review(s) | Add Your Review

Availability: In stock.

Regular Price: $~~14.00~~

Special Price: $8.25

> ▸ Buy 3 for **$7.50** each and *save 10%*
> ▸ Buy 6 for **$6.75** each and *save 19%*

Qty: [   ] Add to Cart OR Add to Wishlist
                                 Add to Compare

Notice that the preceding tier pricing is for users who are not logged in and for users in the General customer group. In the screenshot showing the settings, for some tiers, the Customer Group is set to **NOT LOGGED IN** and for other it is set to **General**. The result is that anonymous visitors, and retail customers who have created an account and logged in, will see these tier prices.

You can see that tiered pricing can be used to change the price depending upon which customer group is viewing the product. An advantage of this method is that it gives you fine control over the pricing. A disadvantage is that it requires you to update the pricing for every product in your catalog, one product at a time.

How to do it...

1. Log in to your site's backend or Administrative Panel.

2. Select **Catalog | Manage Products**. The list of products in your catalog displays.

3. For the product whose tiered pricing you want to set, click on the **Edit** link.

4. Select the **Prices** tab.

5. If the product already has tiered pricing, check which customer groups the pricing applies to. If it applies to **ALL GROUPS**, then be aware that the pricing will apply to the wholesale group. If this is not what you want, then you should change the customer group for the existing tiers.

6. Click on the **Add Tier** button.

7. For the tier you just added, select the website and the Wholesale customer group.

8. Enter the quantity and price for the tier.

9. Save the pricing.

10. Add more tiers as needed.

There's more...

If you are already using tiered pricing, then there is a good chance that some or all of the tiered pricing you set up applies to all groups. You will need to go through your products, looking at the tiered pricing, and ensure that there is no inappropriate pricing applied to the Wholesale customer group.

Catalog price rule

A catalog price rule can be used to apply a discount to a group of products. It can apply to all customers or only to a specific customer group. Use the **Customer Groups** setting, under the **General Information** tab, to select a customer group for the rule:

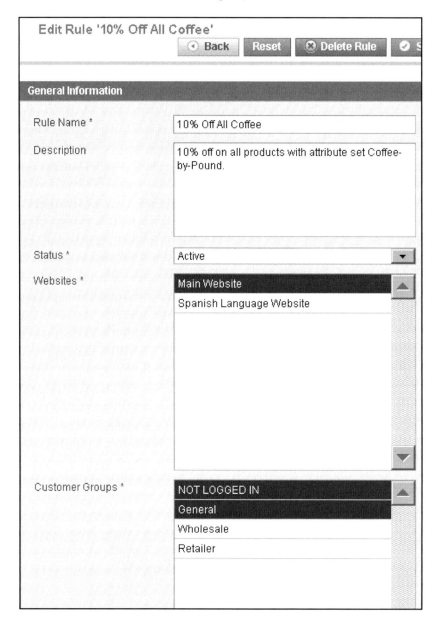

So far, we saw that we could apply a catalog price rule for a specified customer group. Now, how do we apply the price rule to a specified group of products?

If you want to apply a catalog price rule to some of the products in your store, then the usual way of accomplishing this is to apply it to a category or an attribute set. For example, suppose you want to offer a 10 percent discount to retail customers for all coffee products. We would create a catalog price rule that has this condition:

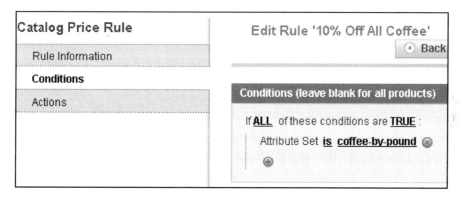

Because all of the coffee products in our store use the attribute set **coffee-by-pound**, this catalog price rule will affect all of the coffee products:

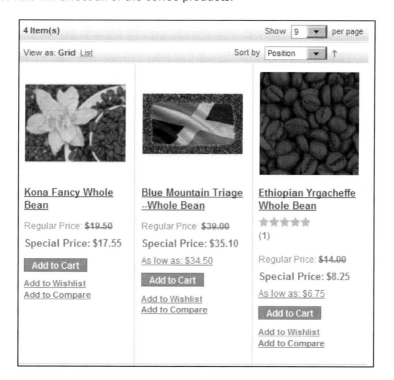

However, for a wholesale store, this might not be appropriate. Because of business considerations, you might want more flexibility and control when applying a discount for your wholesale customers. You might want different discounts for different products. To accomplish this, we will:

> ▸ Create a series of attributes for our products. These attributes will identify the level of discount that wholesale customers will receive.

> ▸ For each product, add the attribute that identifies the level of discount that wholesale customers receive on that product.

> ▸ For each attribute, create a catalog price rule that applies the discount to the products with that attribute.

How to do it...

1. First, we create the attribute that determines what level of discount wholesale customers receive.

2. Log in to your site's backend or Administrative Panel.

3. Select **Catalog | Attributes | Manage Attributes**. The list of attributes in your catalog displays.

4. Click on the **Add New Attribute** button. The **New Product Attribute** page displays:

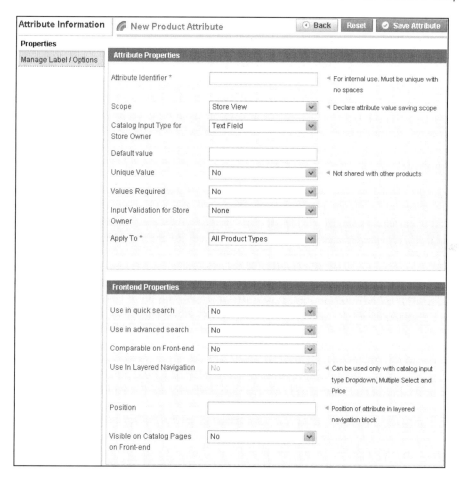

5. There are two tabs on this page—**Properties** and **Manage Label/Options**. You are in the **Properties** tab.

6. The **Attribute Properties** section contains settings that only the Magento administrator (you) will see. These settings are values that you will use when working with the attribute. The **Frontend Properties** section contains settings that affect how this attribute will be presented to your shoppers. We will cover each setting in this section.

7. For **Attribute Identifier**, enter the name that you will use for this attribute. In our example, we will use **wholesale_discount_level**.

8. The **Attribute Identifier** must contain only lowercase letters, numbers, and the underscore character, and it must begin with a letter.

9. The **Scope** of this Attribute can be set to **Store View**, **Website**, or **Global**. Select the one that is appropriate for your business.

10. For **Catalog Input Type for Store Owner**, select **Dropdown**.

11. For **Unique Value**, select **No**.

12. If you select **Yes** for **Values Required**, then you must select or enter a value for this attribute. You will not be able to save a product with this attribute if you leave it blank. If you want to ensure that every single product in your store has a wholesale price, then select **Yes**. Otherwise, select **No**.

13. You can leave **Input Validation for Store Owner** set to the default of **None**.

14. The **Apply To** field determines which product types can have this attribute applied to them. Remember there are several Product Types, including Magento are Simple, Grouped, and Configurable. For wholesale purchases, you might want to limit discounts to **Simple products**.

15. Set all of the **Frontend Properties** to **No**, except for **Use for Price Rule Conditions**. Set that option to **Yes** because the customers will never see or use this attribute.

16. Select the **Manage Labels/Options** tab.

17. Under **Manage Titles,** in the **Admin** field, enter the name that you will use for this attribute in the administrative interface. In our example store, we used **Wholesale Discount Level**.

18. Under the **Manage Options** section, create these options for the attribute:

19. Save the attribute. You are returned to the list of attributes. You should see the one you just added in the list and a success message at the top of the page.

An attribute must be added to an attribute set before it can apply to any products.

1. Select **Catalog | Attributes | Manage Attribute Sets**. The list of attribute sets in your catalog displays.

2. Select the attribute set that you want to contain this new attribute.

3. The attribute should appear in the right-most column, under **Unassigned Attributes**.

4. In the middle column, under **Groups**, scroll until you can see the **Prices** group.

5. Drag the attribute **wholesale_discount_level** (or whatever identifier you gave your attribute) into the **Prices** group and drop it there.

6. Save the attribute set.

7. If needed, repeat this for the other attribute sets in your store.

At this point in the process, you want to select all of the products that will have the same wholesale discount amount. For example, we will select all the products that have a 20 percent discount for wholesale customers.

1. Select **Catalog | Manage Products**. The list of products in your catalog displays.

2. In the first line of the listing, which is shaded, you can enter or select search criteria. Use this to find all of the products that you want to apply the attribute to.

3. Click on the **Search** button. All of the products that meet your search criteria will be listed:

4. At the beginning of each product's line in the list, you see a checkbox. You can either click to select each of the products or use the **Select All** link at the top of that column to select all of the products that showed up in the search. Either way, at this point, you want to select all of products that will have the same discount.

5. After selecting the products that you want to change, from the **Actions** drop-down list, select the **Update attributes**.

6. Click on the **Submit** button. The **Update** attributes page displays.

7. Next to the **Wholesale Discount Level** (or whatever you named the attribute), click the **Change** checkbox.

8. Select the discount level.

9. Save the change.

10. Log in to your store's frontend as a wholesale customer, and test the result.

11. Now you must create a **Catalog Price Rule** that applies the discount to the attribute.

12. Select **Promotions | Catalog Price Rules**.

13. Click on the **Add New Rule** button. The **Rule Information** page displays. You will enter basic information about the rule into this page.

14. Enter the **Rule Name**. Your customers will never see this. This is only so that the site administrator (you) can identify the rule in a list. Make it descriptive so you know what the rule does from the name.

15. Enter the **Description**. It is a good idea to put a plain language summary of the criteria and effect that the rule will have.

16. Use the **Status** field to make the rule **Active**. Later on, you will enter the effective dates for the rule. For the rule to take effect, it must be Active and have an effective date that is in effect now.

17. Select the **Customer Group**(s) to which this rule will apply. We want this to apply only to Wholesale customers:

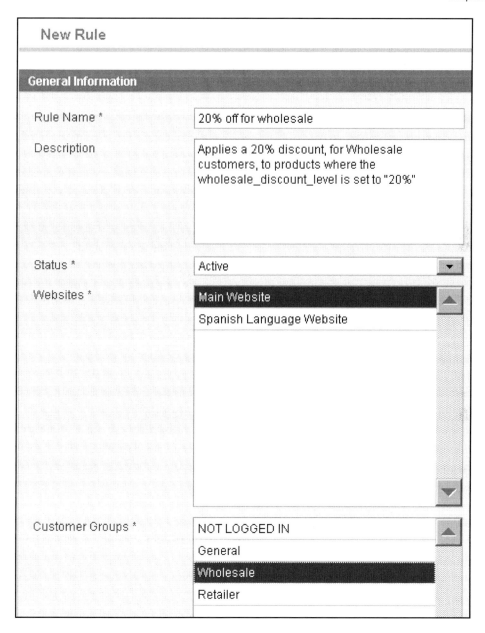

18. Enter the **From Date** and **To Date**. If you leave these blank, the rule will be in effect until you turn it off by making it Inactive.

19. **Priority** determines how this rule will work with other catalog price rules. If several rules apply to the same product, then the one with the higher priority (lower number) will take effect first. Then, the next priority rule will take effect, and so on. This means that you need to keep track of all the catalog price rules that are in effect.

20. Select the **Conditions** tab.

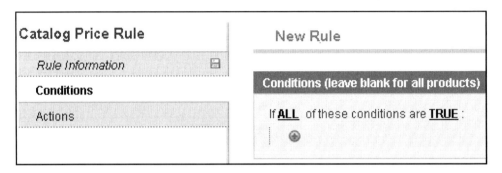

This is where you will enter the filter, which determines which products are affected by the rule.

21. Click on the green plus sign to add a condition:

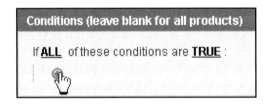

22. A drop-down menu appears, where you will choose the type of condition to add:

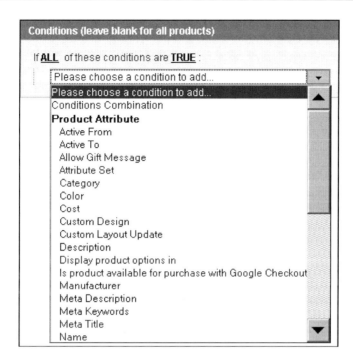

23. For this example, we will choose the attribute that we created. So, we will select **Wholesale_Discount_Level** from the drop-down list:

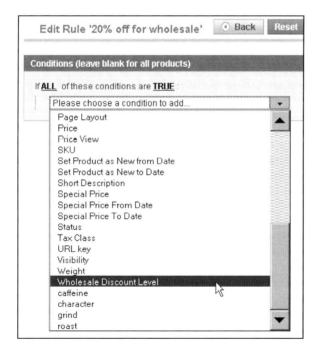

24. Click on the dotted line and then, from the drop-down list, select the value for the attribute:

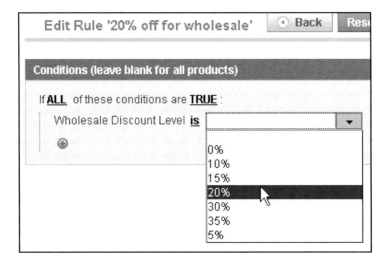

25. Select the **Actions** tab.

26. From the **Apply** drop-down menu, select the type of discount to apply:

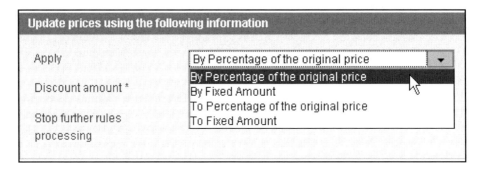

27. To offer a percentage discount, such as "15 percent off the original price", select **By Percentage of the original price**.

28. To offer a dollar amount discount, such as "$10 off the original price", select **By Fixed Amount**.

29. To offer the product at a percentage of its original price, such as "70 percent of the original price", select **To Percentage of the original price**.

30. To offer the product for a fixed dollar amount, such as "All coffee just $8.99 a pound", select **To Fixed Amount**.

31. In **Discount amount**, enter either the amount of the discount, or the discounted price.

If you chose this for the Apply field...	Then enter this into the discount amount field...
By percentage of the original price	The percentage to subtract from the original price.
By Fixed Amount	The dollar amount to subtract from the original price.
To Percentage of the original price	The percentage of the original price that you will charge.
To Fixed Amount	The new sale price.

32. If you select **Yes** for **Stop further rules processing**, then no other catalog price rules will apply to these products.

33. Save the rule.

34. Return to the **Catalog Price Rules** page, and click on the **Apply Rules** button. If you don't do this, then your changes won't apply to your catalog.

35. Preview the results by logging in as a wholesale customer:

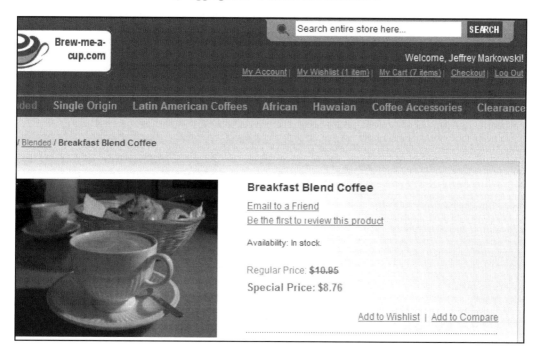

Planning your wholesale strategy

In this chapter, you saw two of the main strategies for creating a wholesale version of your store. Both strategies used customer groups to separate your wholesale customers from your other customers. So, whichever strategy you choose, you will want to:

1. Create a customer group for wholesale customers.

2. Advertise your wholesale program using a static block.

3. Explain your wholesale program using a CMS page.

4. Require wholesale customers to log in to the store, to see the wholesale pricing.

5. Use a tax rule to make all purchases by a wholesale customer non-taxable (depending upon local laws).

After you do these things, you must make a strategic decision: will you use tiered pricing or catalog price rules to offer the wholesale prices? Tiered pricing has the advantage of enforcing a minimum quantity on the wholesale purchases. However, it can take a long time to set up tiered pricing for every item in your catalog.

As you saw in the section on catalog price rules, you can quickly apply a catalog price rule to a large selection of products. However, a catalog price rule cannot require a minimum quantity for purchase.

Index

V

videos
adding, to product pages 70, 71

W

website
creating 222, 223
wholesale customers 241
wholesale store, Magento 241
wholesale strategy
planning 270

Y

Yahoo! 18

Thank you for buying
Magento 1.3 Sales Tactics Cookbook

Packt Open Source Project Royalties

When we sell a book written on an Open Source project, we pay a royalty directly to that project. Therefore by purchasing Magento 1.3 Sales Tactics Cookbook, Packt will have given some of the money received to the Magento project.

In the long term, we see ourselves and you—customers and readers of our books—as part of the Open Source ecosystem, providing sustainable revenue for the projects we publish on. Our aim at Packt is to establish publishing royalties as an essential part of the service and support a business model that sustains Open Source.

If you're working with an Open Source project that you would like us to publish on, and subsequently pay royalties to, please get in touch with us.

Writing for Packt

We welcome all inquiries from people who are interested in authoring. Book proposals should be sent to author@packtpub.com. If your book idea is still at an early stage and you would like to discuss it first before writing a formal book proposal, contact us; one of our commissioning editors will get in touch with you.

We're not just looking for published authors; if you have strong technical skills but no writing experience, our experienced editors can help you develop a writing career, or simply get some additional reward for your expertise.

About Packt Publishing

Packt, pronounced 'packed', published its first book "Mastering phpMyAdmin for Effective MySQL Management" in April 2004 and subsequently continued to specialize in publishing highly focused books on specific technologies and solutions.

Our books and publications share the experiences of your fellow IT professionals in adapting and customizing today's systems, applications, and frameworks. Our solution-based books give you the knowledge and power to customize the software and technologies you're using to get the job done. Packt books are more specific and less general than the IT books you have seen in the past. Our unique business model allows us to bring you more focused information, giving you more of what you need to know, and less of what you don't.

Packt is a modern, yet unique publishing company, which focuses on producing quality, cutting-edge books for communities of developers, administrators, and newbies alike. For more information, please visit our website: www.PacktPub.com.

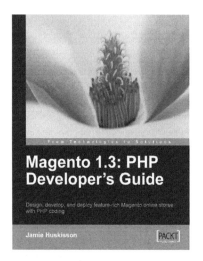

Magento 1.3: PHP Developer's Guide

ISBN: 978-1-847197-42-9   Paperback: 260 pages

Design, develop, and deploy feature-rich Magento online stores with PHP coding

1. Extend and customize the Magento e-commerce system using PHP code

2. Set up your own data profile to import or export data in Magento

3. Build applications that interface with the customer, product, and order data using Magento's Core API

4. Packed with examples for effective Magento Development

Magento 1.3 Theme Design

ISBN: 978-1-847196-64-4   Paperback: 188 pages

Customize the appearance of your Magento e-commerce store with Magento's powerful theming engine

1. Give your Magento stores a unique branded look and feel by creating your own Magento themes

2. Use design techniques to reinforce your brand message and increase sales

3. Customise your Magento theme's look, feel, layout, and features

4. Promote and improve your Magento store with the use of social media such as Twitter, social bookmarks, and so on

Please check **www.PacktPub.com** for information on our titles

Magento: Beginner's Guide

ISBN: 978-1-847195-94-4   Paperback: 300 pages

Create a dynamic, fully featured, online store with the most powerful open source e-commerce software

1. Step-by-step guide to building your own online store

2. Focuses on the key features of Magento that you must know to get your store up and running

3. Customize the store's appearance to make it uniquely yours

4. Clearly illustrated with screenshots and a working example

Selling Online with Drupal e-Commerce

ISBN: 978-1-847194-06-0   Paperback: 264 pages

Walk through the creation of an online store with Drupal's e-Commerce module

1. Set up a basic Drupal system and plan your shop

2. Set up your shop, and take payments

3. Optimize your site for selling and better reporting

4. Manage and market your site

5. This book covers Drupal 5.4

Please check **www.PacktPub.com** for information on our titles

Printed in Great Britain by
Amazon.co.uk, Ltd.,
Marston Gate.